Introduction

Food Finder

Our choice:

INTRODUCTION

Time for Food guides are designed to help you find interesting and enjoyable places to eat in the world's main tourist destinations. Each guide divides the destination into eight areas. Each area has a map, followed by a selection of the restaurants, cafés, bars, pubs and food markets in that area. The aim is to cover the whole spectrum of food establishments, from gourmet temples to humble cafés, plus good food shops or delicatessens where you can buy picnic ingredients or food to cook yourself.

If you are looking for a particular restaurant, regardless of its location, or a particular type of cuisine, you can turn to the Food Finder, starting on page 4. This lists all the establishments reviewed in this guide by name (in alphabetical order) and then by cuisine type.

PRICES

Unlike some guides, we have not wasted space telling you how bad a restaurant is – bad or poor-value restaurants simply do not make it into the guide. Many other guides ask restaurants to pay for their entries, or expect the restaurant to advertise in return for a listing. We do neither of these things: the restaurants and cafés featured here simply represent a selection of places that the author has sampled and enjoyed.

If there is one consistent criterion for inclusion in the guide, it is good value. Good value does not, of course,

mean cheap necessarily. Food lovers know the difference between a restaurant where the high prices are fully justified by the quality of the ingredients and the excellence of the cooking and presentation of the food, and meretricious establishments where high prices are merely the result of pretentious attitudes.

Some of the restaurants featured here are undeniably expensive if you consume caviar and champagne, but even haute cuisine establishments offer set-price menus (especially at lunchtime) allowing budget diners to enjoy dishes created by top chefs and every bit as good as those on the regular menu. At the same time, some of the eating places listed here might not make it into more conventional food guides, because they are relatively humble cafés or takeaways. Some are deliberately oriented towards tourists, but there is nothing wrong in that: what some guides dismiss as 'tourist traps' may be deservedly popular for providing choice and good value.

FEEDBACK

You may or may not agree with the author's choice – in either case we would like to know about your experiences. Any feedback you give us and any recommendations you make will be followed up, so that you can look forward to seeing your restaurant suggestions in print in the next edition.

Feedback forms have been included at the back of the book and you can e-mail us with comments by writing to: *timeforfood@thomascook.com*. No food guide can keep pace with the changing restaurant scene, as chefs move on, establishments open or close, and menus, opening hours or credit card details change. Let us know what you like or do not like about the restaurants featured here. Tell us if you discover shops, pubs, cafés, bars, restaurants or markets that

you think should go in the guide. Let us know if you discover changes – say to telephone numbers or opening times.

Symbols used in this guide

VISA	Visa accepted
Diners Club	Diners Club accepted
MasterCard	MasterCard accepted
🍴	Restaurant
🍷	Bar, café or pub
🧺	Shop, market or picnic site
∅	Telephone
🚇	Transport
❷	Numbered red circles relate to the maps at the start of the section

The price indications used in this guide have the following meanings:

●	budget level
●●	typical/average for the destination
●●●	up-market

FOOD FINDER

▲ Gaudí chocolates

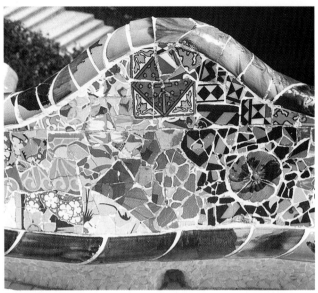

▲ Park Güell

RESTAURANTS BY CUISINE

ALSATIAN
Neichel 77

ARAGONESE
Rincón de Aragón 16

ASTURIAN
Centro Asturiano de
    Barcelona 17

BASQUE
Amaya 9, 17, 76
L'Antull 68
Beltxenea 17, 76
Euskal Etxea 28
San Fermín 51

BRAZILIAN
La Pegui 51
El Rodizio 61

CASTILIAN
El Asador de Aranda 69,
    76
Asador de Burgos 59, 76

CATALAN
Agut d'Avignon 76
L'Antull 68
La Barbacoa de Gràcia
    56, 79
Ca L'Isidre 9, 76
Caballito Blanco 59
Can Cortada 77
Can Culleretes 19
Can Travi Nou 77
Los Caracoles 19
Casa Leopoldo 9
Clàssic Gòtic 20
El Convent 10
La Dama 69, 76
Egipte 10
Estevet 11
La Fonda 20
Garduña 11
Ivan Rey 80
Jaume de Provença 77
Jean Luc Figueras 76,
    80
La Maison du
    Languedoc-
    Roussillon 60
La Marina 50
Petit Paris 69
El Pintor 20, 56
Pitarra 20
Pla de la Garsa 30, 56
Les Quinze Nits 20

El Racó de l'Havanera
    51
Restaurant 7 Portes 41,
    56, 76
Roig Robí 76, 80
Tàbata 81
La Taberna del Cura 56,
    81
El Trobador 56, 71
La Vaquería 71
Via Veneto 71, 76

CHINESE
Dzi 40
Kowloon 60

ECLECTIC
La Flauta Mágica 29, 87
Ot 40
El Pebre Blau 30
Tragaluz 61

FRENCH
Bistrot '106' 59
Brasserie Flo 57
Can Travi Nou 77
La Dama 69, 76
La Maison du
    Languedoc-
    Roussillon 60
Petit Paris 69
Satoru Miyano 70
Via Veneto 71, 76

INDIAN
Govinda 86

IRAQI
Mesopotamia 80

ITALIAN
Giardinetto 57
Lungomare 50
Al Passatore 30, 56
Tramonti '1980' 56, 70

JAPANESE
Salero 31
Sho Jiro 80
Satoru Miyano 70
Tragaluz 61

MALLORCAN
Cal Ricard 17

MEDITERRANEAN
Altillo del Explorador
    68
Ateneu Gastronòmic 19
La Camarga 59
Casa Calvet 59, 76

Gades 29
Gran Café 20
Pla dels Àngels 11
Salero 31
Silenus 11
Taxidermista 21
TNC 57
Vascelum 31

RIOJAN
La Rioja 17

SEAFOOD
Agua 49
Asador del Mar 56
Barceloneta 56
Botafumeiro 56, 76, 79
Cal Pinxo 39
El Cangrejo Loco 49, 56
Can Gotanegra 28
Can Majó 39
Can Ramonet 39
Can Ros 40
Can Solé 40
El Celler del Rocxi 49
Emperador 40
Marina Moncho's 50, 56
Merendero de la Mari 41
La Oficina 41
O'Nabo de Lugo 61
Passadís d'en Pep 29, 76
Els Pescadors 51
El Petit Miau 41, 56
Reial Club Marítim de
    Barcelona 41
El Rey de la Gamba 42,
    51
Salamanca Silvestre 42
Suquet de l'Almirall 42
La Taberna Gallega 51,
    56
Travi Mar 42, 56
El Tunel del Port 52

VEGETARIAN
Biocenter 86
La Buena Tierra 87
Comme-Bio 87
La Flauta Mágica 29, 87
Govinda 86
L'Hortet 11, 86
L'Illa de Gràcia 87
Juicy Jones 87
Self Naturista 87
Sol Solet 87

OTHER
Café Salambo 57
Friends 57
Gaig 77

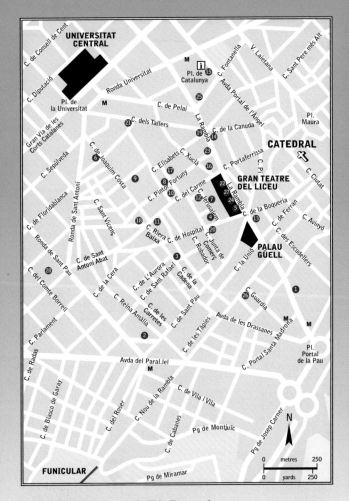

La Rambla and El Raval

La Rambla is the most famous promenade in Spain, an endless parade of street style with flower stalls, pavement cafés and Barcelona's central market. Behind the market, the once seedy El Raval district is changing fast as restaurants and bars spring up around the new Museum of Contemporary Art.

LA RAMBLA AND EL RAVAL
Restaurants

Amaya ❶

La Rambla 20

✆ 93 302 1037

🚇 Metro to Drassanes

Open: daily 1300–1700, 2030–2400

Reservations recommended

All credit cards accepted

Basque

❶❶❶

The down-market location near the foot of La Rambla belies a first-class Basque restaurant, popular with businessmen, politicians and opera singers from the nearby Liceu. The emphasis is on Basque seafood dishes, including lobster, baby eels, sea bream, hake throat and turbot in *txakoli* wine, though meat-eaters will enjoy *morcilla* blood sausage from Bilbao and lamb cutlets Gernika style. In summer there are tables out on the street.

Ca L'Isidre ❷

C. les Flors 12

✆ 93 441 1139

🚇 Metro to Paral.lel

Open: Mon–Sat 1330–1600, 2030–2330

Reservations essential

All credit cards accepted

Catalan

❶❶❶

This intimate, family-run restaurant in the back streets of El Raval is possibly Barcelona's finest, with clients including King Juan Carlos and Catalonia's president Jordi Pujol. Chef César Pastor turns out creative versions of traditional Catalan cuisine, such as tripe with *chorizo* and chickpeas, or pigs' trotters with wild mushrooms and duck liver. The daughter of the owner prepares the desserts, and the meal is accompanied by an excellent all-Catalan wine list.

Casa Leopoldo ❸

C. de Sant Rafael 24

✆ 93 441 3014

🚇 Metro to Liceu

Open: Tue–Sat 1300–1600, 2100–2300, Sun 1300–1600

▲ Amaya

▲ Amaya

Reservations recommended
All credit cards accepted
Catalan
❶❷❸

In the seedy heart of El Raval, this celebrated restaurant serves top-notch Catalan meat dishes with an emphasis on offal, such as oxtail stew, jawbone casserole and tripe with *cap-i-pota* (head and leg). For the less squeamish there are tasty mixed meat and seafood grills, and other unusual specialities including meatballs with cuttlefish and prawns.

El Convent ❹

C. Jerusalem 3
✆ 93 317 1052
🔘 Metro to Liceu
Open: daily 1300–1600, 2000–2400
Reservations recommended
All credit cards accepted
Catalan
❶❷

Wooden panels, antique fittings and tables on the balcony give this popular restaurant behind the market a sense of old-world charm. The food is rustic Catalan, featuring grilled snails, rabbit with *allioli* (garlic mayonnaise) and salt cod with *samfaina*, a Catalan version of ratatouille.

Egipte ❺

La Rambla 79
✆ 93 317 9545
🔘 Metro to Liceu
Open: daily 1300–1600, 2000–2400
Reservations unnecessary
All credit cards accepted
Catalan
❶

This is probably the best value of the many restaurants on La Rambla, with a huge choice of authentic

Catalan dishes on the set menu. The specialities include shellfish gratin, salt cod vol-au-vent, roast chicken, stuffed aubergines and pigs' trotters with prawns.

Estevet

C. Valldonzella 46	
✆ 93 302 4186	
Ⓜ Metro to Universitat	
Open: Mon–Sat 1330–1600, 2100–2400	
Reservations recommended	
All credit cards accepted	
Catalan	
💶💶	

One of the best-loved and most traditional restaurants in Barcelona, with photos of celebrity clients including Gary Lineker and Montserrat Caballé lining the walls. Come here for honest, old-style Catalan cooking, such as stuffed aubergines, duck breast in cheese sauce, and spinach with pine nuts and raisins. Remember to leave some room for the *crema catalana* for dessert.

Garduña

C. Morera 17	
✆ 93 302 4324	
Ⓜ Metro to Liceu	
Open: Mon–Sat 1300–1600, 2000–2400, Sun 1300–1600	
Reservations recommended	
All credit cards accepted	
Catalan	
💶💶	

Situated directly behind La Boqueria market, this bustling Barcelona institution offers hearty Catalan market cuisine using the freshest ingredients. The set lunch menus are particularly good value, featuring large portions of paella, steak and garlic chicken at a very good price.

L'Hortet

C. Pintor Fortuny 32	
✆ 93 317 6189	
Ⓜ Metro to Catalunya or Liceu	
Open: Sun–Thu 1315–1600, Fri–Sat 1315–1600, 2100–2300	
Reservations not allowed	
No credit cards accepted	
Vegetarian	
💶	

A cosy vegetarian restaurant with exposed brick walls and a friendly, laid-back atmosphere. The four-course lunchtime menu is justifiably popular, so it pays to arrive early if you don't want to queue. The menu changes daily but might include soup or a salad buffet, followed by pasta, cauliflower cheese and apple tart, served with water and whole-meal bread.

Pla dels Àngels

C. de Ferlandina 23	
✆ 93 443 3103	
Ⓜ Metro to Catalunya or Universitat	
Open: Mon–Sat 1300–1600, 2030–2400, Sun 1300–1600	
Reservations recommended	
💳💳💳	
Mediterranean	
💶💶	

With tables on the square in front of the contemporary art museum, this place is frequented by the artists, poets and young trendies who are flocking to ultra-hip northern El Raval. The cooking is fresh and simple, featuring pasta dishes, salads and carpaccios, and unusually the good-value set menus are available in the evening and at weekends.

Silenus

C. dels Àngels 8	
✆ 93 302 2680	
Ⓜ Metro to Catalunya or Liceu	
Open: Mon 1300–1600, Tue–Sat 1300–1600, 2100–2330	
Reservations recommended	
💳💳	
Mediterranean	
💶💶	

This funky café-restaurant epitomises the revival of northern El Raval following the opening of the nearby museum. With minimalist décor and modern art on the walls, it is popular with young artists and designers tucking into 'north-south' Mediterranean fusion food such as turkey with mango, chicken with dates and salt cod with aubergine caviar.

LA RAMBLA AND EL RAVAL
Bars, cafés and pubs

Bar Muy Buenas ⓫

C. del Carme 63

⊙ Metro to Liceu or Sant Antoni

Open: Tue–Sat 0800–2100

No credit cards accepted

This beautifully preserved Modernist bar has its original marble counter and splendid wooden furnishings. There is a good selection of *tapas* and *torrades* (toast with various toppings), as well as a lunch menu which might feature paella or spaghetti followed by grilled swordfish or loin of pork.

Bar Ra ⓬

Pl. Gardunya 7

⊙ Metro to Liceu

Open: Mon–Sat 0930–0230

All credit cards accepted

This cool café on a sunny square behind the market is a great place for an al fresco breakfast, with an eclectic menu of muffins, muesli, *tortilla* (potato omelette) and freshly squeezed juices. Later in the day it becomes a trendy student hangout, with laid-back music and a cosmopolitan dinner menu which mixes Mexican, Thai and Mediterranean flavours.

Café de l'Opéra ⓭

La Rambla 74

⊙ Metro to Liceu

Open: daily 0830–0230

No credit cards accepted

This splendid Modernist coffee-house opened in 1929 and has been frequented by artists, intellectuals and politicians ever since. You can sit inside with a newspaper beneath the dark wood and panelled mirrors, or take a seat on the pavement watching the world go by. The pastries here are irresistible.

Café Moka ⓮

La Rambla 128

⊙ Metro to Catalunya or Liceu

Open: daily 0800–2300

All credit cards accepted

George Orwell witnessed a Civil War shoot-out here from a rooftop across the street, and the café which he wrote about in *Homage to Catalonia* is still going strong, with fading film

▲ Café de l'Opéra

posters on the walls and a simple menu of pizzas, paellas, *tapas* and grills.

El Corte Inglés

Pl. de Catalunya 14

Ⓜ Metro to Catalunya

Open: Mon–Sat 1000–2130

All credit cards accepted

Ten floors of shopping heaven lead up to the top-floor café inside Barcelona's biggest department store. The main attraction here is the rooftop terrace, with bird's-eye views over the city's main square. There is also a more formal restaurant offering sophisticated regional cuisine.

Granja Viader

C. Xuclà 4

Ⓜ Metro to Liceu

Open: Mon 1700–2045, Tue–Sat 0900–1345, 1700–2045

No credit cards accepted

Barcelona's *granjas* (milk bars) are just the place for a thick hot chocolate and early-evening pastry during the long wait for supper. This is one of the oldest, founded in 1870, and also features a shop selling fresh farmhouse produce such as organic milk, yoghurt and curd cheese.

Mamacafé

C. Doctor Dou 10

Ⓜ Metro to Catalunya

Open: Mon 0900–1700, Tue–Fri 0900–0100, Sat 1300–0100

Funky music and colourful modern designs make this a popular hangout with the in crowd who are currently drawn to El Raval. The cooking is modern fusion food with several vegetarian choices along with more standard offerings such as grilled salmon.

Muebles Navarro

C. de la Riera Alta 4

Ⓜ Metro to Liceu or Sant Antoni

Open: Sun and Tue–Thu 1700–2400, Fri–Sat 1700–0200

No credit cards accepted

This Manhattan-style bar is situated in an old furniture showroom where the customers sit around on sofas and chaises longues. A good place for a late-night drink, it also serves plates of cheese and ham, as well as the house special, New York lox (smoked salmon).

Pans & Company

La Rambla 123

Ⓜ Metro to Catalunya

Open: Sun–Thu 0900–2400, Fri–Sat 0900–0300

No credit cards accepted

This popular sandwich chain with branches across the city has got fast food down to a fine art, offering fresh baguettes spread with tomato and top-quality fillings such as *tortilla* (potato omelette), smoked salmon and cured ham.

Rita Blue

Pl. Sant Agustí 3

Ⓜ Metro to Liceu

Open: Mon–Fri 1100–0200, Sat–Sun 1800–0200

A sure sign of the changes sweeping through El Raval, this cool designer bar features Latin music, Tex-Mex cuisine, fish-shaped mirrors and a vaguely minimalist style. Come here for a full meal or a drink and a snack, from nachos and *fajitas* to anchovies with *focaccia* bread.

LA RAMBLA AND EL RAVAL
Shops, markets and picnic sites

Shops

Asia Food Superstore ㉑

C. dels Tallers 27

🔵 Metro to Catalunya or Universitat

Open: Mon–Sat 0930–1400, 1600–2100

No credit cards accepted

Although El Raval used to be known as the 'Barrio Chino' (Chinatown), it is only recently that it has acquired a large immigrant population. If you tire of olive oil and Spanish ham, this shop serves the local Chinese community with imported products ranging from soy sauce, rice wine and chilli paste to tinned bamboo shoots and ready-made *dim sum*.

▲ Escriba

Casa Guitart ㉒

La Rambla 95

🔵 Metro to Liceu

Open: Mon–Sat 0900–1400, 1700–2000

This deli on the edge of La Boqueria market features cheeses from all over Spain, plus haunches of ham and speciality sausages from Burgos, Salamanca and Mallorca. Among other items on sale are tinned anchovies, truffles, saffron, nougat and a selection of Spanish brandies in miniature bottles.

Champion ㉓

La Rambla 113

🔵 Metro to Catalunya

Open: Mon–Sat 0915–2115

This large central supermarket is a good place for stocking up on everyday items. There is a takeaway counter at the entrance selling spit-roast chicken and chips, along with specialities such as grilled rabbit and steaming mounds of paella.

El Corte Inglés ⑮

Pl. de Catalunya 14

🔵 Metro to Catalunya

Open: Mon–Sat 1000–2130

All credit cards accepted

Barcelona's biggest department store has a supermarket in the basement as well as the **Club del Gourmet**, a delicatessen featuring cheeses, hams, fresh fish, ready-cooked dishes, Catalan specialities and wines from the various regions of Spain.

Escriba ㉔

La Rambla 83

🔵 Metro to Liceu

Open: daily 0830–2100

Most people are drawn to this pastry-shop by its magnificent mosaic façade, one of the finest examples of Modernist art on La Rambla. The displays inside the shop are no less impressive, with heavenly pastries and handmade chocolates presented in elegantly wrapped gift boxes. There is also a small café at the back.

Marks & Spencer ㉕

Pl. de Catalunya 32

🔵 Metro to Catalunya

Open: Mon–Sat 1000–2130

All credit cards accepted

This well-known British department store has opened a flagship branch on Barcelona's main square. The food hall in the basement

▲ La Boqueria

sells all the standard British staples, such as sliced bread, baked beans, piccalilli and liquorice allsorts, to a mixture of curious Catalans and homesick Brits.

Torres – La Bolsa de los Licores 26

C. Nou de la Rambla 25

 Metro to Liceu or Drassanes

Open: Mon–Sat 0900–1200, 1600–2030

The 'liquor stock exchange' is a crowded neighbourhood shop where the customers are locals rather than tourists. It sells fresh produce and everyday foodstuffs, but is most notable for the bottles of wines and spirits lining the shelves, including a fine selection of miniatures and several unusual liqueurs.

Markets

La Boqueria 27

La Rambla 91

Metro to Liceu

Open: Mon–Sat 0800–2100

Barcelona's biggest market is housed in a 19th-century market hall on La Rambla. The entire place is a feast for the eyes, from hanging hams and sausages to colourful fruit and vegetable stalls featuring the freshest tomatoes, aubergines and peppers. Fish and seafood stalls are arranged in a circle at the centre, and there are other stalls devoted to olives, eggs and dried

fruit, as well as stand-up *tapas* bars offering beer and tripe for breakfast. The best way to enjoy the market is just to wander at random, but it is worth seeking out a couple of stalls at the back – **Petras** (No 869–870), which specialises in wild mushrooms, and **La Masia de la Boqueria** (No 970), which features pork products from pigs raised on the farmers' own farms.

Mercat de Sant Antoni 28

Metro to Sant Antoni

Open: Mon–Sat 0800–1400, 1700–2000

Many people prefer this market to La Boqueria, as it has more of a neighbourhood feel. The emphasis is very much on fresh produce, from strings of tomatoes and fat pork chops to huge slabs of salt cod and tuna.

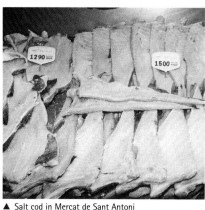

▲ Salt cod in Mercat de Sant Antoni

Spanish regional cuisine

A matter of origins

The cooking of Spain is regional cuisine, rooted in the landscape, climate and history of the various regions. Even a dish like paella, which to many is synonymous with Spain, has its origins in Valencia where the Arabs first introduced rice. The Madrileños have their *cocidos*, hearty stews swimming with meat, cabbage and chickpeas, the Basques have their hake and cod, the Andalusians have their *gazpacho*, and the Catalans have their *crema catalana* (burnt custard) and *suquet de peix* (fish casserole).

All of these dishes rely heavily on the quality of the raw ingredients for their success. As a general rule, the Spanish do not go in for excessive flavourings, just a little garlic, some fresh herbs, some tomatoes and olive oil. The skill which goes into creating a perfectly executed meal does not begin in the kitchen, but in the soil. People want to know how their fish was caught, where their peppers were grown, what was the diet of the pig that went to make the ham. These things matter far more than a fancy sauce whipped up by the chef to mask the flavour of an inferior product. That is why the Spanish take a fierce regional pride in the quality of their produce, and why, while foreigners judge a paella by the amount of seafood on top, what really matters to a Valencian is the quality of the rice.

ARAGÓN
The historic kingdom of Aragón was once joined to Catalonia, and its cooking reflects its shared position at the foot of the Pyrenean mountains. Among the items on offer at **Rincón de Aragón** (*C. Carme 28; ✆ 93 302 6789;* 🚇 *metro to Liceu;* ❸❸) are Teruel ham, kid with peppers, roast lamb, fried breadcrumbs and *chorizo* cooked in wine.

ASTURIAS
Asturias is part of Spain's Celtic fringe, a land of bagpipes, coal

▲ Outdoor paella

miners and green hills which is far removed from most people's image of the country. The food reflects the harsh winter climate, and the best-known dish is *fabada asturiana*, a casserole of pork, blood sausage and white beans. You can try it accompanied by a glass of fizzy Asturian cider at the **Centro Asturiano de Barcelona** (*Passeig de Gràcia 78; ✆ 93 215 3010;* Ⓜ *metro to Diagonal or Passeig de Gràcia;* ⓔ).

BASQUE COUNTRY

Along with Catalonia, the Basque Country is considered the culinary centre of Spain. Basque cooking relies heavily on seafood, and the Basques eat more fish per head than any other nation on earth. Salt cod features in many dishes, a legacy of the Basque tradition of seafaring. Classic dishes include *merluza a la vasca* (hake in white wine sauce), *bacalao a la vizcaina* (salt cod with peppers) and *kokotxas* (fritters of hake throat). You can try traditional Basque cooking at **Amaya** (*see page 9*, or a more refined version at **Beltxenea** (*C. Mallorca 275; ✆ 93 215 3024;* Ⓜ *metro to Diagonal or Passeig de Gràcia; closed Sat lunch and Sun;* ⓔⓔⓔ), a discreet and intimate town house with a brass plaque at the entrance, which gives little clue that this is the top Basque restaurant in Barcelona.

▲ Tortilla

> **People want to know how their fish was caught, where their peppers were grown, what was the diet of the pig that went to make the ham.**

MALLORCA

Although the cooking of the Balearic islands is similar to that of Catalonia, there are various local specialities such as *trempo* (summer salad), *tumbet* (Mallorcan ratatouille) and *sobrasada* (spicy pork sausage), all of which are available at **Cal Ricard** (*C. Francisco Giner 21; ✆ 93 217 0605;* Ⓜ *metro to Diagonal; closed Sat lunch and Sun;* ⓔⓔ).

RIOJA

Spain's best-known wine-producing region has a distinctive style of cuisine, and any dish cooked *a la riojana* will contain the red peppers for which the region is famous. Specialities include slow-roasted lamb, stuffed peppers, *menestra de verduras* (sautéed vegetables) and potatoes with peppers and *chorizo*. You can try all of these, along with Rioja wines, at **La Rioja** (*C. Duran i Bas 5; ✆ 93 301 2298;* Ⓜ *metro to Urquinaona;* ⓔⓔ).

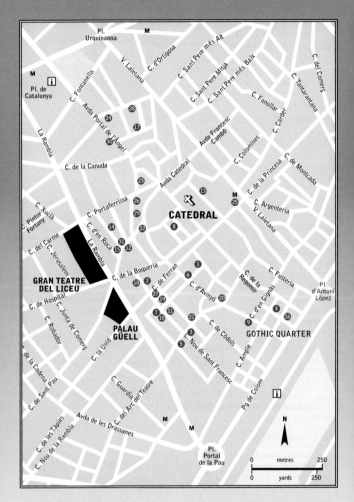

Barri Gòtic

The oldest part of Barcelona is known as the Barri Gòtic (Gothic Quarter). The narrow streets around the cathedral, with their small, specialist shops, make a great place for strolling, while the restaurant scene is increasingly concentrated in the lower half of the Barri Gòtic where it sweeps down towards the sea.

BARRI GÒTIC
Restaurants

Ateneu Gastronòmic ❶

Pas de l'Ensanyança 2

✆ 93 302 1198

🚇 Metro to Jaume I

Open: Mon–Fri 1330–1530, 2030–2330, Sat 2030–2330

Reservations recommended

All credit cards accepted

Mediterranean

€€

The 'gastronomic academy' behind the city hall turns out inventive Mediterranean cuisine with a distinct Portuguese accent discernible in dishes such as coriander and garlic soup or steak with myrtle and thyme. Among the more unusual choices are horse tartare, kangaroo fillet with *foie gras*, Moroccan wood-pigeon *pastilla* and a Moscatel sorbet infused with Havana cigars.

Can Culleretes ❷

C. Quintana 5

✆ 93 317 3022

🚇 Metro to Liceu

Open: Tue–Sat 1330–1600, 2100–2300, Sun 1330–1600

Reservations recommended

Catalan

€€

The oldest restaurant in Barcelona was founded in 1786 and continues to trade on its old-world image. The speciality here is seafood (the tasting menu includes half a grilled lobster) but there are also Catalan meat classics, such as *botifarra* sausage with beans and chicken with *samfaina* sauce.

Los Caracoles ❸

C. dels Escudellers 14

✆ 93 302 3185

🚇 Metro to Liceu or Drassanes

Open: daily 1300–2400

Reservations recommended

All credit cards accepted

Catalan

€€

The most famous restaurant in Barcelona cultivates an old-fashioned image, with ceramic tiles, wine butts and photos of celebrity customers on the walls.

▲ Los Caracoles

Chickens are spit-roasted out on the street, and you walk through the kitchen with its steaming mounds of paella and snails. Definitely a tourist trap, but still worth a visit for its authentic, traditional Catalan cuisine.

Clàssic Gòtic

C. Plata 3
☏ 93 319 9298
Ⓜ Metro to Drassanes
Open: daily 1900–2400
Reservations recommended
💳 💳
Catalan
❸❻

This stylish restaurant, in a 16th-century Gothic building where Picasso once had a studio, features creative combinations such as chicken breasts in malt whisky, sole with roasted hazelnuts and suckling pig in anchovy cream.

La Fonda ❺

C. dels Escudellers 10
☏ 93 301 7515
Ⓜ Metro to Liceu or Drassanes
Open: daily 1300–1530, 2030–2330
Reservations not allowed
💳 💳 💳
Catalan
❻

The queues outside testify to the popularity of this restaurant, which offers fresh Catalan cuisine in a bright, open-plan setting, with tables spread over two floors. Locals prefer this to **Los Caracoles** (*see page 19*) on the same street, and it is certainly better value if not so atmospheric.

Gran Café ❻

C. d'Avinyó 9
☏ 93 318 7986
Ⓜ Metro to Jaume I or Liceu
Open: daily 1300–1630, 2000–0030
Reservations recommended
All credit cards accepted
Mediterranean
❻❻

This elegant Modernist café has been restored to its original splendour, with wooden ceilings and balconies and a live pianist in the evenings. Politicians from the nearby city hall come here to enjoy fresh market cuisine, such as grilled snails, paella, black rice and steak with *foie gras* – as well as more unexpected offerings like cold cockle and lychee soup.

El Pintor ❽

C. Sant Honorat 7
☏ 93 301 4065
Ⓜ Metro to Jaume I or Liceu
Open: daily 1300–1645, 2000–0130
Reservations recommended
All credit cards accepted
Catalan
❻❻

One of the best of the restaurants around the cathedral, this serves modern Catalan market cuisine in an old town house with wood-beamed ceilings and exposed brick walls. Among the specialities are cod with honey and raisins, salmon tartare with armagnac, and duck breast with strawberry sauce.

Pitarra ❾

C. d'Avinyó 56
☏ 93 301 1647
Ⓜ Metro to Drassanes
Open: Mon–Sat 1330–1600, 2030–2300
Reservations recommended
💳 💳 💳
Catalan
❻❻

This renowned old restaurant has been given a new lease of life in the up-and-coming nightlife district down towards the port. The chef has won awards for his highly personal creations, such as carpaccio of salmon with sheeps' cheese and wild boar in chocolate sauce. There is a strong emphasis on game in season.

Les Quinze Nits ❼

Pl. Reial 6
☏ 93 317 3075
Ⓜ Metro to Liceu
Open: daily 1300–1545, 2030–2330
Reservations not allowed
All credit cards accepted
Catalan
❻

This busy restaurant on one of Barcelona's most attractive squares has pioneered the concept of offering simple, fresh Catalan cuisine at excellent prices. Starters include Catalan salad and carpaccio of salt cod, while main courses might be grilled fish or steak with roquefort. The only problem is that bookings are not taken and at weekends the queue can stretch right across the square. Get here early if you want one of the outdoor tables.

Taxidermista ⑩

Pl. Reial 8
✆ 93 412 4536
🚇 Metro to Liceu
Open: Tue–Sun 1330–1600, 2030–2400
Reservations recommended
💳 💳 American Express
Mediterranean
€ €

A trendy designer bistro in an old taxidermist's studio, with a cavernous cellar and tables out on the square. The menu features modern Catalan and Mediterranean dishes, such as lamb couscous, salt cod with yucca crisps and duck breast with truffle vinaigrette. If you don't want a full meal, there are *tapas* at the bar as well as ice creams ranging from dark chocolate to papaya and tequila sorbet.

▲ Taxidermista

BARRI GÒTIC
Bars, cafés and pubs

4Gats ⑰

C. Montsió 3

Ⓜ Metro to Urqinaona

Open: Mon–Sat 0900–0200,
Sun 1700–0200

All credit cards accepted

You can pay homage to
Barcelona's artists at
this Modernist tavern,
once the bohemian
meeting place of Picasso
and his friends. The
restaurant at the back is
somewhat overpriced,
but to soak up the
atmosphere all you need
to do is pop into the
front bar for a sandwich
and a beer.

Ambos Mundos ⑪

Pl. Reial 10

Ⓜ Metro to Liceu

Open: Wed–Mon 0930–0200

🔲 💳 American Express

This popular tourist
choice makes a great
spot for people-
watching on an attrac-
tive square. You can sit
outside at tables

beneath the arcades
enjoying anything from
croissants or eggs and
bacon for breakfast, to
tapas and more
substantial meals served
in terracotta bowls.

Bar del Pi ⑫

Pl. Sant Josep Oriol 1

Ⓜ Metro to Liceu

Open: Mon–Sat 0900–2300,
Sun 1000–1500, 1700–
2200

No credit cards accepted

A bustling bar at the
corner of two pretty
squares, where buskers
play and artists set up
stalls at weekends.
During the evening, the
action spills out on to
the square as office
workers stop by for a
beer and a plate of ham
on their way home.

Café d'Estiu ⑬

Pl. Sant Iu 5

Ⓜ Metro to Jaume I

Open: Apr–Sept, Tue–Sun
1000–2200

No credit cards accepted

This charming summer
café is situated in the
Gothic courtyard of the
former royal palace,
now shared between
two neighbouring
museums. The setting is
perfect, especially when
candlelit at night, and
the café serves a simple
menu of sandwiches,
snacks and pastries.

Granja Dulcinea ⑭

C. Petritxol 2

Ⓜ Metro to Liceu

Open: daily 0900–1300,
1630–2100

No credit cards accepted

The best-known *granja*
in Barcelona has
wooden furnishings and
white-jacketed waiters
serving up old-
fashioned treats such as
sponge fingers dipped in
hot chocolate. For
anyone with a sweet
tooth, this makes a
great place to stop for a
mid-morning break or
an early-evening snack.

Irati ⑮

C. Cardenal Casañas 17

Ⓜ Metro to Liceu

Open: Tue–Sat 1200–2400,
Sun 1200–1630

🔲 💳 American Express

There is barely room to
move in here during the

▲ Bar del Pi

▲ 4Gats

early evening, when trays of *pintxos* (Basque *tapas*) are laid out along the bar. You can help yourself, but remember to keep a tally by counting the cocktail sticks on your plate. When you've gorged yourself on snacks and Basque cider, you can always move to the restaurant at the back, which serves excellent Basque meat and seafood dishes.

La Plata 16

C. de la Mercè 28
⊙ Metro to Drassanes
Open: Mon–Sat 1000–1600, 2000–2300
No credit cards accepted

This small tiled bar is one of several *tascas* along this street, traditional sailors' bars serving cider and wine from the barrel, along with fried sardines, *chorizo* in cider and pungent Asturian *cabrales* (blue cheese). Some of these places appear a little rough at the edges but they are great fun and full of atmosphere.

Sushi-Ya 18

C. Quintana 4
⊙ Metro to Liceu
Open: daily 1300–1600, 2030–2330
No credit cards accepted

Japanese food has arrived in Barcelona and this place offers Japanese '*tapas*' such as fried noodles, croquettes and chicken sticks, along with sushi of salmon, tuna and octopus and a set menu of sushi, salad and *miso* soup.

La Taberna Real 19

C. les Heures 6
⊙ Metro to Liceu
Open: Mon–Sat 1330–1630, 2000–2400
💳 💳

This fashionable new eatery is all plain white furniture and chic minimalist design. The food follows the same minimalist theme, with simple but delicious cheese plates from the various regions of Spain, as well as selections of Catalan sausages and cold meats.

Venus 20

C. d'Avinyó 25
⊙ Metro to Jaume I
Open: Mon–Sat 1200–2400
No credit cards accepted

A buzzy, alternative café, run by two sisters and popular with young artists, travellers and gays. The menu features cheap international snacks, such as cous-cous, moussaka and vegetarian lasagne, together with salads and sandwiches, all of which are served throughout the day.

BARRI GÒTIC
Shops, markets and picnic sites

Shops

Art Escudellers

C. dels Escudellers 23

⦿ Metro to Liceu or Drassanes

Open: daily 1100–2300

All credit cards accepted

This extraordinary emporium resembles a ceramics warehouse, with its street-level floor devoted to pottery from every corner of Spain. Go down into the cellar and there is an excellent wine vault, as well as a wine bar and a shop selling high-quality food products such as ham, cheese and olive oil.

Caelum ㉒

C. de la Palla 8

⦿ Metro to Liceu

Open: Tue–Sat 1000–1400, 1700–2030, Sun 1000–1400, Mon 1700–2030

This unusual shop sells only foodstuffs that have been produced in monasteries, including wine and liqueurs, sweets, biscuits and rose-petal jam.

Casa Colomina ㉓

C. Cucurulla 2 (also at C. Portaferrissa 8)

⦿ Metro to Liceu

Open: Mon–Sat 1000–1400, 1600–2030

This famous producer of *turrón* (almond nougat) has been in business since 1908. The *turrón*, made at a factory in Alicante and exported around the world, comes in several unusual flavours including bitter chocolate, *crema catalana* and candied fruits.

Casa del Bacalao ㉔

C. Comtal 8

⦿ Metro to Urquinaona

Open: Mon–Sat 0900–1500, 1730–2030

No credit cards accepted

Few outsiders can understand the appeal of dried salted cod, but it remains an essential ingredient in Catalan and Basque cooking. Apart from a few extras such as tomatoes, garlic and olive oil, the 'house of cod' sells little else. Just remember, if you do buy some cod, it must be soaked overnight to remove the salt before cooking.

La Colmena ㉕

Pl. de l'Àngel 12

⦿ Metro to Jaume I

Open: daily 0900–2100

No credit cards accepted

Gateaux and cream tarts fill the window display at this tempting cake shop, along with almond biscuits and sweet treats

▲ *Turrón* from Casa Colomina

such as nougat, coffee caramels and chocolate-covered nuts. There are also savoury pies with fillings ranging from *sobrasada* (Mallorcan pork sausage) to *foie gras*.

Fargas 26

Pl. Cucurulla 12

🅟 Metro to Liceu

Open: Mon–Fri 0900–1330, 1600–2000, Sat 0930–1400, 1600–2000

American Express

They still use a millstone to grind the powder at Barcelona's best-known chocolate shop, which sells gift-wrapped boxes of dark chocolates, bonbons and candied fruits.

Herboristeria del Rei 27

C. Vidre 1

🅟 Metro to Liceu

Open: Mon–Sat 1000–1400, 1700–2000

This old-fashioned herbalist's was founded in 1818 and there are still banks of old wooden drawers lining the walls. It's worth going in just to take a look, but you can also buy herbal teas, saffron, cinnamon sticks, dried herbs and various herbal remedies.

Mel Viadiu 28

C. Comtal 20

🅟 Metro to Urquinaona

Open: Mon–Sat 1000–1400, 1630–2030

All credit cards accepted

▲ Fargas

Open since 1898, this shop specialises in all kinds of honey, with flavours ranging from chestnut and orange blossom to rosemary and eucalyptus. There are honeys with ginseng and royal jelly, and also honey-flavoured sweets.

La Pineda 29

C. del Pi 16

🅟 Metro to Liceu

Open: Mon–Sat 0900–1500, 1700–2200, Sun 1100–1500, 1900–2200

All credit cards accepted

Hams and sausages hang from butcher's hooks on the ceiling in this timeless delicatessen, which also functions as a *bodega* with wine from the barrel and a handful of marble tables and wooden stools at the back of the shop.

Planelles-Donat 30

Avda Portal de l'Àngel 25

🅟 Metro to Catalunya

Open: Mon–Sat 1000–1400, 1600–2000

No credit cards accepted

Another shop specialising in *turrón*, an almond sweetmeat flavoured with honey and cinnamon which probably dates back to the Arab occupation of Spain. You can buy it ready-boxed to give as a present, or treat yourself to a slab sold by weight at the counter.

> Markets

Plaça del Pi 31

🅟 Metro to Liceu

Open: first and third weekend of each month: Fri–Sun 1100–1400, 1700–2100

Twice a month, producers of honey, chocolate, bread, pastries and farmhouse cheeses set up their stalls at an artisan food market on the square.

Catalan specialities

Enjoying the simple things in life

CALÇOTS

If you are driving in Catalonia between January and April and you come across a farmhouse restaurant with cars parked outside, smoke rising from the chimney and a chalked sign advertising a *calçotada*, stop. You are in for a treat. The reason for all this excitement is the annual harvest of *calçots*, spring onions the size of leeks which are a speciality of Tarragona province, south of Barcelona. In Barcelona itself you will see *calçots* on the menu in season, usually as a starter, but for the full experience you have to head out into the countryside and join in the *calçotada* feast.

The onions are barbecued over vine cuttings until they are black, then brought to the table on terracotta tiles. Everyone is issued with a bib and a bowl of *romesco* sauce, a fiery concoction of hazelnuts, almonds, tomatoes, garlic and olive oil. The idea is to peel the skin off with one hand and hold the *calçot* in the other, dipping it into the sauce then tipping back your head as you lower the vegetable into your mouth. After a few minutes your fingers are black and your chin is dripping pink, but nobody cares as they all look the same. Lamb chops and sausages are grilled over the embers, ice cream and cake are brought out

to follow, and enormous quantities of *cava* are drunk. When you have been to a *calçotada* you understand what it means when people say that the Catalans know how to appreciate the simple pleasures of life.

MAR I MUNTANYA

Do you fancy chicken with lobster? Rabbit with snails? Pigs' trotters with prawns? Welcome to Catalonia. Apart from a predilection for eating those parts of the animal which foreigners often prefer to ignore, the Catalans have a gift for creating the most unlikely combinations of ingredients and making them work. This characteristic style of cooking is known as *mar i muntanya* ('sea and mountain'), and most commonly features meat and seafood not just on the same plate, but cooked together in a way that would be unthinkable in most culinary traditions. Thus *sípia amb mandonguilles* is a casserole of cuttlefish and meatballs, blackened by the cuttlefish ink, while *pollastre amb gambes* is chicken stuffed with shrimps. If you want to see this approach taken to extremes, seek out *calamars farcits amb salsa de xocolata*, which is squid stuffed with minced pork and served in a chocolate sauce. Apparently it was a firm favourite of the artist

Salvador Dalí, which probably explains a lot.

PA AMB TOMÀQUET

The Catalan passion for taking the good things in life and enjoying them in all their simplicity is perfectly illustrated by *pa amb tomàquet* (also known as *pan con tomate* in Spanish). What could be simpler than a piece of crusty bread, rubbed with tomato, sprinkled with salt and drizzled with olive oil? Yet this dish, an essential component of every Catalan meal, has become central to the Catalan cultural identity. It is what Catalans dream about when they are far from home, and when immigrants to Barcelona start rubbing tomato on their bread you know that they have arrived. Entire books have been written about bread with tomato, the Catalan comfort food *par excellence*.

It has to be said that it is quite delicious. Toasted on a barbecue, with baskets of tomatoes and garlic and a bottle of oil on the table so that you can make your own. Topped with *escalivada* (roasted vegetable salad) and anchovies or thin slices of ham or cheese. On its own. Dipped in *allioli*. Whatever you prefer, a piece of *pa amb tomàquet* is a taste of Catalonia, of sunshine and olive groves and Mediterranean skies. Once you have tasted this, you will never want to look at a slice of bread and butter again.

> **Everyone is issued with a bib and a bowl of romesco sauce, a fiery concoction of hazelnuts, almonds, tomatoes, garlic and olive oil.**

▲ *Pa amb tomàquet*

El Born

This former maritime trading district has become the most happening part of town, with an eclectic range of restaurants and bars which are busy well into the night. This is the best place to take part in the 'tapeo', an early-evening tapas crawl with a distinct Basque theme which has taken Barcelona by storm.

EL BORN
Restaurants

Can Gotanegra ❶

C. Sant Antoni Sombrerers 3
Ø 93 319 5371
Ⓜ Metro to Jaume I
Open: Tue–Sat 1300–1600, 2030–2330, Sun 1300–1700

Reservations recommended

[card icons]

Seafood

❷❷

This small, smart seafood restaurant is hidden away in a back alley behind the church of Santa Maria del Mar. There are a few meat dishes but the emphasis is on fish, from black rice and baked sea bass to a platter of grilled seafood, and a tasting menu which features everything from seafood salad to grilled prawns and mussels in white wine.

Euskal Etxea ❷

Plaçeta de Montcada 1
Ø 93 310 2185
Ⓜ Metro to Jaume I
Open: Tue–Sat 1300–1530, 2100–2330

Reservations recommended

[card icons]

Basque

❷❷

Although this Basque bar and cultural centre is best known for its *pintxos* (see page 47), it is also worth a visit for a full sit-down meal. The menu features Basque classics such as T-bone steaks and *bacalao pil-pil* (salt cod in garlic sauce), accompanied by Basque cider or wine from the Rioja Alavesa vineyards.

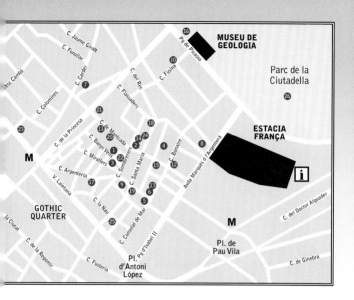

La Flauta Mágica ❸

C. Banys Vells 18

✆ 93 268 4694

🚇 Metro to Jaume I

Open: daily 2100–2400

Reservations recommended

[VISA] [＝＝] [⌾]

Eclectic-Vegetarian

❻❻

This funky New Age restaurant typifies the changing nature of this area, offering vegetarian cooking with attitude. Dishes such as rose-petal omelette with *sake* betray a Japanese influence, and banana leaves stuffed with jasmine rice has a hint of Indonesia about it. Although most of the dishes are vegetarian, there are also

one or two made with organic meat.

Gades ❹

C. Esparteria 10

✆ 93 310 4455

🚇 Metro to Jaume I

Open: Mon–Thu 2030–2430, Fri–Sat 2030–0130

Reservations recommended

[VISA] [＝＝] American Express

Mediterranean

❻❻

This trendy new bistro is very popular at week-ends, so go during the week if you want a quiet meal. The emphasis is on simple, fresh cuisine, such as carpaccios of tuna, salmon and ostrich or selections of pâté and cheese. Another

speciality is a fondue of *boeuf bourgignonne* with a plate of chips for dipping.

Passadís d'en Pep ❺

Pl. del Palau 2

✆ 93 310 1021

🚇 Metro to Barceloneta or Jaume I

Open: Mon–Sat 1330–1530, 2100–2330

Reservations recommended

All credit cards accepted

Seafood

❻❻❻

This celebrated restaurant makes no attempt to attract passing trade, but aficionados of good seafood cooking know where to find it. It is hidden down an unmarked corridor beside a bank and you have to ring on the doorbell to be let in. There is no menu, just superb fresh seafood cooked according to the whim of the chef and whatever is in the market that day.

Al Passatore

Pl. del Palau 8

✆ 93 319 7851

Ⓜ Metro to Barceloneta or Jaume I

Open: daily 1300–0100

Reservations not allowed

VISA

Italian

€

An extremely popular Italian restaurant offering wood-fired pizzas and authentic Italian cuisine. Among the specialities are fresh pasta, aubergine with Parmesan, and home-made tiramisu for dessert. The lunch menu has three courses plus wine and coffee, all for the price of a pizza.

El Pebre Blau ❶

C. Banys Vells 21

✆ 93 319 1308

Ⓜ Metro to Jaume I

Open: Thu–Tue 2100–2400

Reservations essential

VISA

Eclectic

€€

This buzzy new designer restaurant takes fusion food to extremes, with a menu mixing Mediterranean, Indian and even Irish flavours. Among the specialities are Moroccan turkey and date *tajine*, Keralan chicken with coconut, and a smoked salmon roulade flambéed in whisky.

Pla de la Garsa ❼

C. Assaonadors 13

✆ 93 315 2413

Ⓜ Metro to Jaume I

Open: Mon–Sat 1300–1600, 2000–0100, Sun 2000–0100

Reservations recommended

VISA ◐ American Express

Catalan

€€

This converted stables is full of old-world charm, with marble tables, ceramic-tiled walls and a wrought-iron spiral staircase leading to the upstairs dining room. The speciality is a plate of cold cuts, pâtés and cheeses, but cooked dishes are also available and there is a good-value lunch menu which unusually includes a cheese course before dessert.

Salero ⑧

C. del Rec 60

℘ 93 319 8022

◉ Metro to Barceloneta or Jaume I

Open: Mon–Fri 1330–1600, 2100–2400, Sat 2100–0100

Reservations recommended

VISA

Mediterranean-Japanese

€€

The stark white walls of this former tuna-salting warehouse bring a touch of New York style to Barcelona, attracting a hip young crowd for dinner and late-night drinks. The cooking is Japanese-inspired, with dishes such as tuna tartare, sardine *tempura* and *kakiage* (sautéed squid with courgettes and carrot), as well as fresh takes on Catalan classics such as a delicious duck breast with mango.

▲ Passadís d'en Pep

Vascelum ⑨

Pl. Santa Maria 4

℘ 93 319 0167

◉ Metro to Jaume I

Open: Tue–Sun 1230–1600, 2000–2400

Reservations recommended

VISA ◐

Mediterranean

€€

With tables on the square in summer and views of Santa Maria church, this makes a very pleasant lunch spot. The menu features everything from Basque-style casseroles of salt cod to Catalan rabbit with snails, along with pasta and more sophisticated offerings such as duck breast with bilberry sauce.

EL BORN
Bars, cafés and pubs

Café Kafka 🔟

C. Fusina 7

🅟 Metro to Jaume I or Arc de Triomf

Open: Mon–Sat 1300–1600, 2000–2400

This industrial-looking bar close to Ciutadella Park epitomises the trend for Manhattan-style chic among a young, hip and gay crowd in El Born. Chefs from Sudan and the Philippines turn out cheap Middle-Eastern and Oriental dishes such as hamburgers, falafel, houmous and chop suey.

Café Textil 🔟

C. de Montcada 12

🅟 Metro to Jaume I

Open: Tue–Sun 1000–2400

The café in the court-yard of the **Textile Museum** makes a lovely place to relax, sunny and shady by day and candlelit at night. The menu features snacks such as sandwiches, pastries and ice cream, as well as more interna-tional choices like Caesar salad, Greek salad, aubergine pâté and guacamole with nachos.

Cal Pep 🔟

Pl. Olles 8

🅟 Metro to Barceloneta or Jaume I

Open: Mon 2000–2400, Tue–Sat 1315–1615, 2000–2400

All credit cards accepted

The aroma of fresh seafood hits you as you walk in the door of this crowded *tapas* bar. You sit at the long counter watching owner Pep Manubens frying up prawns, sardines and squid to order, and directing regular customers to whatever is freshest that day. There is a small restau-rant out at the back, but eating at the bar is a lot more fun.

Estrella de Plata 🔟

Pl. del Palau 9

🅟 Metro to Barceloneta or Jaume I

Open: Mon–Fri 1300–1600, 2030–2400

No credit cards accepted

This former sailors' bar has been reinvented as a place serving 'designer *tapas*', such as squid in balsamic vinegar or *foie gras* in port. There is no menu and are no prices, you simply point to what you want or listen to the waiters calling out the choices. Some of the city's top chefs gather here on Monday

VINS I PLATILLOS

la Vinya del Senyor

PLAÇA SANTA MARIA, 5
08003 BARCELONA
TEL. 93 310 33 79

evenings to chew the fat on their day off. With the opening hours matching those of restaurants, this bar is an exception to the general rule that *tapas* do not make a meal.

Euskal Etxea 14

Plaçeta de Montcada 1

🚇 Metro to Jaume I

Open: Tue–Sat 1200–2330, Sun 1300–1530

The pioneer of the Basque *tapas* craze which is sweeping Barcelona, this crowded Basque cultural centre is at its best soon after 1930 in the evening, when around 40 varieties of *pintxos* are laid out on the bar. These tempting titbits might feature mushroom *tortilla*, salt cod with *allioli*, roquefort with walnuts or smoked salmon with peppers, neatly arranged on small pieces of bread. They are best accompanied by *trakoli*, a gently sparkling wine from the Basque Country, or by fizzy Basque cider, poured from a great height. Be warned that although *pintxos* are not supposed to be a substitute for an evening meal, they are very moreish and can be an expensive way of eating out.

Golfo de Bizkaia 15

C. Vidrieria 12

🚇 Metro to Jaume I

Open: Tue–Sat 1330–1530, 2030–2330, Sun 1330–1530

The *pintxos* are replaced throughout the evening at this heaving Basque bar, where fishcakes, croquettes and sausages appear from the kitchen as quickly as you can eat them. There is also a restaurant featuring numerous varieties of salt cod as well as bowls of garlic prawns and enormous T-bone steaks.

Hivernacle de la Ciutadella 16

Passeig de Picasso

🚇 Metro to Arc de Triomf

Open: daily 1000–0100

All credit cards accepted

Situated inside an iron-and-glass greenhouse

▲ Sweet almond biscuits

on the edge of Ciutadella Park, this charming café with its covered terrace makes a great place for a drink at any time of year. There are simple meals such as soup, salads and grilled meat, and occasional concerts are held.

Sagardi

C. Argenteria 62

🔵 Metro to Jaume I

Open: daily 1200–2400

All credit cards accepted

The action spills out on to the square at this lively Basque bar, where the cider is poured from over the shoulder and the wine comes out of a cask in the wall. The selection of *pintxos* here is one of the best, and there is also a restaurant featuring grilled fish and steaks and other Basque specialities.

La Taverna del Born ⑱

Passeig del Born 27

🔵 Metro to Jaume I

Open: Tue–Sun 1100–0100

Cashing in on the craze for Basque cooking in this part of town, this busy bar serves grills, steaks and casseroles, as well as lunchtime and early-evening *pintxos*. With tables out of doors on an attractive promenade, it makes a good vantage point on summer evenings.

Va de Vi ❸

C. Banys Vells 16

🔵 Metro to Jaume I

Open: daily 1200–1500, 1700–0100

All credit cards accepted

These wine vaults inside a 16th-century Gothic palace make a civilised,

if expensive, place for an apéritif or after-dinner drink. You sip *cava* or Rioja by candle-light beneath stone arches, and nibble on delicate morsels of cheese and Iberian ham.

La Vinya del Senyor ⑲

Pl. Santa Maria 5

🔵 Metro to Jaume I

Open: daily 1200–2400

All credit cards accepted

The wine bar opposite Santa Maria del Mar has a huge choice of wines, sherries and *cavas* by the glass as well as tasty nibbles ranging from olives and *pa amb tomàquet* to plates of anchovies and cured ham. In summer this makes the perfect place to meet for a pre-dinner drink, with wooden tables outside on the square.

Xampanyet ⑳

C. de Montcada 22

🔵 Metro to Jaume I

Open: Tue–Sat 1200–1600, 1830–2330, Sun 1200–1600

Barcelona's original champagne bar is still the best place to begin a *tapeo* before moving on to the trendier Basque joints. With marble tables, tiled walls and antique wine barrels on the floor, this is a classic. Along with *cava*, the speciality is fresh cider, accompanied by anchovies and tomato bread.

EL BORN
Shops, markets and picnic sites

Shops

Brunells ㉑

C. de la Princesa 22

🅜 Metro to Jaume I

Open: Mon–Sat 0830–1430, 1600–2000, Sun 0830–1500

No credit cards accepted

This well-known pastry-shop is famous for its chocolate creations, as well as *turrón* (nougat) and sweet almond biscuits. You can try some of the cakes in the neighbouring café on C. Montcada.

Casa Gispert ㉒

C. Sombrerers 23

🅜 Metro to Jaume I

Open: Mon–Fri 0900–1330, 1600–1930, Sat 1000–1400, 1700–2000

💳 💳 💳

If you go into one food shop in Barcelona for the sheer pleasure of browsing, this should be the one. Sacks of dried fruit and nuts spill on to the floor, the scent of coffee hangs in the air, and almonds are still roasted in the original wood oven, in service since 1851. With jars of olives and drawers full of saffron and cinnamon, this place has all the feel of an oriental bazaar.

Comme-Bio ㉓

V. Laietana 28

🅜 Metro to Jaume I

Open: Mon–Sat 0900–2300, Sun 1200–2300

All credit cards accepted

The health food shop attached to this vegetarian restaurant is a good place for picking up picnic food, such as bread, pastries, pizzas, organic fruit, cheeses, yoghurts and several varieties of tofu. It also sells organic wine.

Tot Formatge ㉔

Passeig del Born 13

🅜 Metro to Jaume I

Open: Mon–Fri 0800–1300, 1630–1930, Sat 0900–1300

No credit cards accepted

One of the best cheese shops in Barcelona features regional Spanish cheeses such as Idiazabal from the Basque Country, blue *cabrales* from Asturias, goats' cheese from Extremadura and ewes'

milk cheese from the Catalan Pyrenees.

Vila Viniteca ㉕

C. dels Agullers 7

🅜 Metro to Jaume I

Open: Mon–Sat 0800–1500, 1700–2100

All credit cards accepted

This third-generation family-run wine shop has a huge range of Spanish and Catalan wines, with knowledgeable staff who will guide you through the maze and point you in the right direction.

Picnic sites

Parc de la Ciutadella ㉖

🅜 Metro to Arc de Triomf or Jaume I

Barcelona's best-known park, Parc de la Ciutadella, is a short walk from this district and makes a pleasant place for a picnic among the fountains, statues and landscaped gardens.

▲ Parc de la Ciutadella

Catalan wine

A growing reputation

Although restaurants offer a wide choice of wines from regions such as Rioja and Ribeira del Duero, you should take the opportunity while in Barcelona of trying the local Catalan wines. Catalonia is one of Spain's leading wine regions, producing a good variety of whites and reds in addition to sparkling *cava*. These days Catalan wines are enjoying a growing reputation, as producers turn to grape varieties such as Cabernet Sauvignon and Chardonnay to supplement the more traditional native grapes.

CAVA

The Catalan version of champagne is much cheaper than the real thing and makes a great wine for a celebration. It was first produced in 1872, using the French *méthode champenoise*, in response to the devastation of the Catalan vineyards by the phylloxera plague. Traditionally made from local grape varieties such as Parellada, Macabeo and Xarello, it is fermented in steel tanks and a second time in the bottle, where it is aged for up to five years. These days, more and more producers are using the Chardonnay grape to create a premium *cava*. Some 90 per cent of all *cava* production takes place in the small town of Sant Sadurni d'Anoia, west of Barcelona. The largest producer, Codorniu, turns out a staggering 30 million bottles of *cava* each year. Their leading brands are **Ne Plus Ultra**, made with native grapes, and **Anna de Codorniu**, made with Chardonnay. Another top producer is **Freixenet**, whose black-label *cava* is widely exported and instantly recognisable. It is also worth seeking out *cavas* from some of the smaller, lesser-known wineries, such as Juvé i Camps, Mas Tinell and Josep Maria Raventós. For the best selection of *cavas* in Barcelona, visit **Xampany** (*see page 65*).

PENEDÈS

Cava is produced in the Penedès region, Catalonia's foremost area of wine production. The main town of this region is Vilafranca del Penedès, home to the Torres wine dynasty. Any wine made by **Torres** is likely to be reliable, though they range from the everyday to the truly magnificent. **Viña Sol** is a popular, fruity white, made from the Parellada grape, bottled young and available everywhere. **Gran Viña Sol** is a more complex version, blended with Chardonnay, while **Fransola** is a single-estate Sauvignon Blanc aged in oak. The 'house red' is the full-bodied **Sangre de Toro**, though if you can afford it you should really try one of Torres' serious reds. **Gran Coronas** is an oak-aged blend of Cabernet

Sauvignon and Tempranillo, while the flagship **Mas La Plana** is a single-estate Cabernet which has been compared favourably in blind tastings with the very best clarets. It is expensive, but not for what it is. Other reliable producers from this region include Rene Barbier and Bach.

PRIORAT
The rising star of Catalan wine production is the Priorat region of Tarragona, an area of chalky slopes and steeply terraced vineyards which creates some of the most highly prized red wines in Spain. These full-bodied wines have a high alcoholic content, typically 14 per cent but sometimes as much as 18 per cent, and are the perfect accompaniment to roast or grilled meat. One of the best names is **Scala Dei**, the monastery where vines in this area were first planted. Others to look out for include **De Muller** and **Rocafort de Queralt**. With its current popularity, the Priorat cannot produce enough wine to satisfy demand, and wines from this area attract a premium price.

> **The flagship Mas La Plana is a single-estate Cabernet which has been compared favourably in blind tastings with the very best clarets.**

OTHER AREAS
Among other wine denominations in Catalonia, look out for:
- **Alella** – fruity, dry whites such as those produced by Marqués de Alella
- **Conca de Barberà** – an up-and-coming area for full-bodied reds
- **Costers del Segre** – especially the red wines from Castell del Remei and Raïmat, who also produce a Chardonnay-based *cava* at their estate near Lleida
- **Empordà** – for light rosé wines, the young red Vi Novell and the slightly fizzy Blanc Pescador, which goes well with fish
- **Terra Alta** – powerful dark reds from Tarragona province, similar in style to Priorat.

WHERE TO BUY WINE
The mark-up on wine in most Barcelona restaurants is not great so you can experiment with Catalan wines at a reasonable price. To buy some to take home, try the gourmet club of **El Corte Inglés**, or shops like **Art Escudellers** (*see page 24*), **Vila Viniteca** (*see page 35*) and **Colmado Quilez** (*see page 64*). Another shop with an excellent selection is **Vines i Caves la Catedral** (*Pl. Ramon Berenguer el Gran 1;* ⊙ *metro to Jaume I*). The best wines are those labelled *crianza* or *reserva*, which have been aged in oak barrels for specified periods.

▲ Torres wines

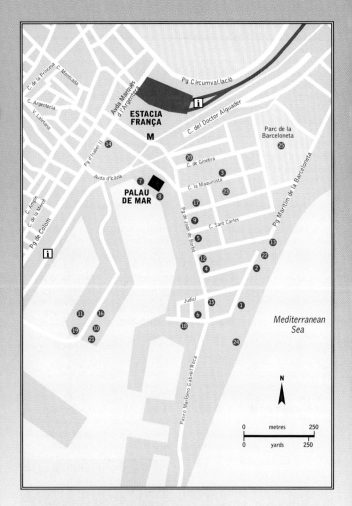

Barceloneta and Port Vell

The old fishing village of Barceloneta has long been famous for its seafood restaurants and the chiringuitos (kiosks) which used to offer simple meals on the beach. With new beaches and promenades, this area has seen sweeping changes in recent years, and tapas bars now line the waterfront on the site of the old harbour.

BARCELONETA AND PORT VELL
Restaurants

Cal Pinxo ❶

C. Baluard 124

✆ 93 221 5028

🚇 Metro to Barceloneta

Open: Tue–Sat 1230–1600, 2030–2330, Sun 1230–1600, also Mon in summer

Reservations recommended

All credit cards accepted

Seafood

€€€

The best known of the *chiringuitos* (beach bars) has been given a new lease of life as a smart seafood restaurant with a large summer terrace. Authors, politicians and footballers come here at weekends to enjoy classic rice and seafood dishes such as grilled spiny lobster, razor clams and sea bass baked in a salt crust. A second branch of Cal Pinxo is situated in the Palau de Mar, a restored warehouse with several seafood restaurants on a sunny terrace beside the harbour.

Can Majó ❷

C. Almirall Aixada

✆ 93 221 5455

🚇 Metro to Barceloneta

Open: Tue–Sat 1300–1600, 2030–2330, Sun 1300–1600

Reservations recommended

All credit cards accepted

Seafood

€€€

This famous restaurant started out as a *chiringuito* (beach bar) and has stayed in the same family for 30 years, but it now serves sophisticated dishes such as black rice, lobster paella and mixed grills of fish and seafood. You can start with a *pica-pica* of prawns, fried fish, seafood croquettes and baby squids in their own ink, followed by simply grilled fish or one of several varieties of paella.

Can Ramonet ❸

C. la Maquinista 17

✆ 93 319 3064

🚇 Metro to Barceloneta

Open: Mon–Sat 1000–1600, 1930–2330, Sun 1000–1600

Reservations recommended

All credit cards accepted

Seafood

€€

The oldest building in Barceloneta has tables beneath parasols on a pretty market square, and upturned wine barrels for tables at the bar. You can snack on a selection of fishy *tapas*, or splash out on a platter of grilled seafood with own-label *cava* in the more formal restaurant at the back. A local institution, and deservedly so.

▲ Port Vell

▲ La Oficina

Can Ros ❹

C. Almirall Aixada

✆ 93 221 4579

🚇 Metro to Barceloneta

Open: daily 1300–1700, 2000–2400, closed Wed eve

Reservations recommended

🔲 💳 American Express

Seafood

€€

Typical of the old-style restaurants of Barceloneta, this place offers top-quality seafood at very reasonable prices in a back-street dining room just off the promenade. Start with an assortment of fish *tapas* followed by lobster paella or black rice, or try the varied evening tasting menu which includes such delights as seafood salad, cauliflower stuffed with prawns, and salt cod with langoustines.

Can Solé ❺

C. Sant Carles 4

✆ 93 221 5012

🚇 Metro to Barceloneta

Open: Tue–Sat 1300–1600, 2000–2300, Sun 1300–1600

Reservations recommended

🔲 💳

Seafood

€€€

This famous restaurant started out as a tavern in 1903 and still has its original beer pumps and marble tables. The tourists tend to miss it as it is not on the seafront, but locals know it as one of the best places to eat in Barceloneta. Popular dishes include black rice with *allioli* and salt cod with honey, and the restaurant is reputed to be the birthplace of the Catalan fish stew known as *sarsuela*.

Dzi ❻

Passeig de Joan de Borbó 76

✆ 93 221 2182

🚇 Metro to Barceloneta

Open: daily 1300–1600, 2000–2400

Reservations recommended

🔲 💳 American Express

Chinese

€€

If you fancy something different, this restaurant serves contemporary Chinese cuisine along with some Singaporean and Thai dishes. Sea bream and prawns are served up in Chinese styles, and the meat dishes include veal with mango. In summer you can eat outside on a terrace beside the port.

Emperador ❼

Pl. de Pau Vila 1

✆ 93 221 0220

🚇 Metro to Barceloneta

Open: daily 1300–2300

Reservations recommended

All credit cards accepted

Seafood

€€

With tables in the sun on a harbourside terrace, this makes a great place for a long and lazy lunch. The menu is more tourist-oriented than many of the restaurants in Barceloneta, featuring steamed mussels, carpaccio of salmon, swordfish kebabs and sole meunière, as well as paellas, noodle casseroles, oven-baked fish and steak au poivre. Another advantage is that it stays open throughout the day so you do not have to eat at Spanish mealtimes if you do not want to.

Merendero de la Mari ❽

Pl. de Pau Vila 1

✆ 93 221 3141

🅜 Metro to Barceloneta

Open: Mon–Sat 1300–1600, 2030–2330, Sun 1300–1600

Reservations recommended

All credit cards accepted

Seafood

€€€

The daughter of Pinxo of **Cal Pinxo** (*see page 39*) fame has opened her own seafood restaurant, with tables by the sea on the terrace of the ultra-trendy Palau de Mar. The specialities include salt cod puffs and anglerfish in tomato sauce, as well as

sole in orange juice and black noodles with clams. The desserts here are a treat, ranging from *crema catalana* to cinnamon mousse flavoured with rose essence.

La Oficina ❾

Passeig de Joan de Borbó 30

✆ 93 221 4005

🅜 Metro to Barceloneta

Open: Wed–Mon 1300–1630, 2030–2330

Reservations unnecessary

All credit cards accepted

Seafood

€

With checked table-cloths and views of the sea, this has all the feel of an old-style fishermen's bar. There are special menus featuring lobster paella or an assortment of grilled seafood, but the best deal here is the lunchtime set menu, which might include salad or hors d'oeuvres followed by grilled octopus or the fresh fish of the day.

El Petit Miau ❿

Moll d'Espanya

✆ 93 225 8110

🅜 Metro to Barceloneta or Drassanes

Open: daily 0900–0200

Reservations recommended

All credit cards accepted

Seafood

€€

This popular restaurant inside the Maremagnum complex is successfully attempting to recreate

the atmosphere of the early 20th century, with Modernist décor and an abundance of wrought iron and stained glass. 'The Little Kitten' serves everything from *tapas* and a children's menu to seafood grills and a 'symphony' of salt cod, and the tables by the window have a marvellous view of the sea.

Reíal Club Marítim de Barcelona ⓫

Moll d'Espanya

✆ 93 221 6256

🅜 Metro to Barceloneta or Drassanes

Open: Mon–Sat 1330–1600, 2100–2330, Sun 1330–1630

Reservations recommended

All credit cards accepted

Seafood

€€€

You may feel out of place without your own boat at this elegant restaurant belonging to Barcelona's yacht club. Turning its back on the Maremagnum mall, the restaurant looks towards the city, with tables on a terrace overlooking the marina. The chef combines traditional Catalan cooking with innovative seafood dishes, such as salmon with *wasabi* (Japanese horseradish), sea bream with rosemary and langoustine kebabs with parmesan.

Restaurant 7 Portes ⓮

Passeig Isabel II 14

☎ 93 319 3033

🚇 Metro to Barcelona

Open: daily 1300–0100

Reservations unnecessary

All credit cards accepted

Catalan

💶💶

One of the oldest restaurants in Barcelona was founded in 1836 and was the first establishment in the city to have gaslights and running water. Che Guevara, Federico García Lorca and Joan Miró are among those to have eaten here and enthused about its tiled floor, white-clad waiters and traditional Catalan cuisine. Among the specialities are 'blind man's paella' (without bones), lobster *bouillabaisse* and chicken with prawns, as well as a different rice dish for every day of the week. A few tables are reservable but at busy times you may have to queue.

El Rey de la Gamba

Passeig de Joan de Borbó 46–53

☎ 93 225 6400

🚇 Metro to Barceloneta

Open: daily 1200–0030

Reservations unnecessary

💳 💶

Seafood

💶💶

The 'king of the prawn' occupies two huge restaurants which take up almost an entire block of the seafront promenade. Starters

include garlic prawns, live clams, oysters and barnacles, followed by seafood paella, grilled fish or a *suquet* casserole of white fish with potatoes. The portions are large, designed for two people to share, though half-portions are available on request.

Salamanca Silvestre ⑬

C. Almirante Cervera 34

☎ 93 221 5033

🚇 Metro to Barceloneta

Open: daily 1300–1600, 2000–2300

Reservations recommended

All credit cards accepted

Seafood

💶💶

This lively seafront restaurant recreates the atmosphere of the *chiringuitos* (beach bars) with an outdoor terrace facing the beach. The emphasis is on seafood – live clams, grilled prawns, a *pica-pica* of fried fish – but there is also Castilian-style roast kid, and a *tapas* bar with hams hanging from the ceiling. The recommended dessert is lemon sorbet, served with *marc de champagne*.

Suquet de l'Almirall ⑮

Passeig de Joan de Borbó 65

☎ 93 221 6233

🚇 Metro to Barceloneta

Open: Tue–Sat 1300–1600, 2100–2300, Sun 1300–1600

Reservations recommended

💳 💶

Seafood

💶💶💶

The best of the restaurants along the promenade achieves a fine balance between traditional Catalan seafood dishes and modern creativity. The specialities are rice dishes, such as *paella 4 octubre* (made with lobster and *samfaina* sauce) and the *suquet* casserole of the restaurant's name, made here with sea bream and prawns. The tasting menu consists of six fish dishes followed by a lobster *fideuà* (noodle paella), and for meat-eaters there is *foie gras* in Pedro Ximenez sherry. The wine list is one of the finest in Barcelona.

Travi Mar ⑯

Moll d'Espanya

☎ 93 225 8136

🚇 Metro to Barceloneta or Drassanes

Open: daily 1300–0100

Reservations recommended

All credit cards accepted

Seafood

💶💶

The seafood branch of a well-known chain of restaurants is situated inside the Maremagnum complex overlooking the port. As well as paella, noodle casseroles and plain grilled fish, the specialities include sea bass with Jabugo ham.

BARCELONETA AND PORT VELL
Bars, cafés and pubs

Can Ganassa ⑰
Pl. Barceloneta

🚇 Metro to Barceloneta

Open: Thu–Tue 0900–2400

All credit cards accepted

This locals' bar on the old main square has an enormous variety of *tapas* laid out along the bar and huge pots of mussels steaming away in the kitchen. Another speciality is *torrades*, slices of toast rubbed with tomato and topped with anchovies, ham or *allioli*.

Casa Juanito ⑱
C. Escar 7

🚇 Metro to Barceloneta

Open: Mon–Sat 1300–1600, 2000–2300

This small, attractive fishermen's bar has

▲ Tapas Bar Maremagnum

blue-checked tablecloths and a simple menu of cod, hake, paella and fishy *tapas* at very reasonable prices. It is situated right beside the fishing harbour, so the fish is fresh off the boats.

El Chipirón 19

Moll d'Espanya

🔴 Metro to Barceloneta or Drassanes

Open: daily 1200–0100

All credit cards accepted

Situated at the entrance to the Maremagnum mall, this large seafood restaurant offers paella, black rice and grilled lobster as well as sea bass and sea bream baked in a salt crust. Most people, though, prefer to take a table on the sunny waterfront terrace and tuck into *tapas* of oysters, prawns, mussels, anchovies and squid.

El Lobito 20

C. Ginebra 9

🔴 Metro to Barceloneta

Open: Mon–Sat 1200–1600, 2100–2400

To catch the flavour of old Barceloneta, head

for this crowded fishermen's bar where the locals wade through huge plates of fresh seafood – there is barely a tourist in sight.

El Palau del Pollastre 12

Passeig de Joan de Borbó 50

🔴 Metro to Barceloneta

Open: Tue–Sun 1300–2100

No credit cards accepted

If you want to eat in Barceloneta but you don't like seafood, this cheap-and-cheerful place on the promenade offers takeaway chicken and chips and a simple menu of soup, salads and jacket potatoes.

Tapas Bar Maremagnum 21

Moll d'Espanya

🔴 Metro to Barceloneta or Drassanes

Open: daily 1100–0100

All credit cards accepted

One of the best of the Spanish-style *tapas* bars which have sprung up in Barcelona over the last few years. With tables in the sun on a harbourside terrace, this is a great place for a plate of ham, some garlic potatoes, a slice

of *pa amb tomàquet* and a beer. Vegetarian *tapas* are clearly marked on the menu, and there is a special tasting menu with a selection of *tapas* for two people to share.

La Tasca de la Vasca 10

Moll d'Espanya

🔴 Metro to Barceloneta or Drassanes

Open: Mon–Sat 1000–2400, Sun 1200–2400

No credit cards accepted

This Basque bar on the first floor of Maremagnum serves a selection of *pintxos* as well as Basque-style casseroles of garlic prawns, mushrooms and salt cod. The downside is that you have to eat inside a shopping mall rather than out in the fresh air with a view of the sea.

La Venta Manchega 22

C. Guíter 58

🔴 Metro to Barceloneta

Open: daily 1030–2300

No credit cards accepted

This tiny place facing Barceloneta beach has just a few outdoor tables and is the nearest thing left to the old-style *chiringuitos* (beach bars) which were closed down in the early 1990s. It features a simple menu of grilled sardines, octopus, paella and fresh fish dishes, and closes down for the day 'when it gets cold'.

BARCELONETA AND PORT VELL
Shops, markets and picnic sites

Markets

Mercat de la Barceloneta ㉓

C. Andrea Dòria

🚇 Metro to Barceloneta

Open: Mon–Thu and Sat 0900–1400 and Fri 0900–1400, 1630–2000

Every district of Barcelona has its own neighbourhood market and this one retains its fishing-village atmosphere, with several stalls specialising in fresh fish. Much of this comes from the fish auctions which take place twice a day (early morning and late afternoon) when the catch comes in at the fishing harbour at the end of C. Escar.

Picnic sites

Barceloneta Beach ㉔

🚇 Metro to Barceloneta

Barceloneta Beach makes a great spot for a picnic, and there are benches along the seafront promenade.

Parc de la Barceloneta ㉕

🚇 Metro to Barceloneta

Parc de la Barceloneta is one of Barcelona's more unusual parks, with an old water tower and gasometer incorporated into the design.

▲ Mercat de la Barceloneta

Tapas bars

Plugging the gap between meals

Tapas have their origin in the old Spanish custom of placing a free *tapa* (lid) of food over a drink. It may only have been a slice of ham or a small saucer of olives, but it fulfilled two important functions – it allowed the proprietor to display a measure of generosity to his customers, and it gave the thirsty customer something to eat with his drink. The Spaniards do not like to drink without food, and especially they do not like to get drunk. *Tapas* allow people to drink all evening but still stay sober because every glass of wine is accompanied by a mouthful of *tortilla* or a salt cod croquette.

Nowadays, of course, *tapas* are rarely free, though there are still bars where you will be offered a few crisps, olives or roasted almonds with your drink. Instead, *tapas* have metamorphosed into a branch of Spanish cuisine, with staples such as *albondigas* (meatballs), *callos*

(tripe), *caracoles* (snails), *gambas* (prawns), *ensaladilla rusa* (Russian salad) and *patatas bravas* (spicy potatoes) available at bars up and down the country. What many visitors fail to realise is that *tapas* were never meant to be a substitute for a meal. By all means go in a crowd and order a dozen plates to share, but it will be a very expensive way of eating out. *Tapas* were designed to plug the gaps between meals.

Another point to make about *tapas* is that they are not especially Catalan. The last few years has seen an explosion of *tapas* bars in Barcelona, similar to that which took place in London and other cities in the 1980s, but purists scoff at the arrival of this foreign import. True, Barcelona has always had its sailors' *tascas*, such as **La Plata** (*see page 23*) and several others in the same street, including **La Celta** (*C. Mercè 16*), a bustling *pulpería* where chunks

of octopus and squid are washed down with Galician white wine. And there has always been a handful of old-style Spanish *tapas* bars, where trays of meatballs and tripe were displayed beneath the counter and a *tortilla* stood on the bar, you pointed to what you wanted and the barman took it away and heated it up in a microwave. These places still exist, and a good example is **El Roble** in Gràcia (*see page 83*).

What has changed in Barcelona is the arrival of bright, modern *tapas* bars, bursting on to the scene down by the waterfront and along Passeig de Gràcia. Typical of this new style is **Tapas Bar Maremagnum** (*see page 44*), one of a chain of bars which have made *tapas* trendy. In truth they appeal more to foreigners than to locals, but even the people of Barcelona can now be seen by the harbour, eating *tapas* and drinking beer in place of a more conventional meal. Another stylish place, which pre-dates the *tapas* craze, is **Cervecería Catalana** (*C. Mallorca 236;* ⓜ *metro to Diagonal or FGC to Provença; open: daily 1000–0200*), where two long counters are covered with everything from grilled prawns and crab croquettes to deep-fried peppers and roasted vegetable salad.

The other big trend in Barcelona is the craze for the *txikiteo*, the early-evening *tapas* crawl imported from the Basque Country. From 1900 onwards, groups of friends wander from bar to bar, drinking Basque cider or *txakoli* wine and nibbling on *pintxos*. These bite-sized snacks are essentially small pieces of bread topped with anything from smoked salmon to Idiazabal cheese or miniature pork kebabs. All are priced equally, and the idea is to help yourself from the bar and keep a tally by counting the cocktail sticks on your plate. The best places to try *pintxos* are **Irati** (*see page 22*) and **Euskal Etxea** (*see page 28*), though there are numerous other places in the Born district. Two good Basque *tapas* bars in L'Eixample are **Taktika Berri** (*see page 83*) and **Txestatu** (*C. Consell de Cent 329;* ⓜ *metro to Passeig de Gràcia; open: daily 0800–0130*). Near here is a branch of **Lizarran** (*C. Mallorca 257*), a popular Basque *tapas* chain which also has branches in Gràcia (*see page 83*) and the Barri Gòtic (*C. Dr Joaquim Pou 2*).

> **Tapas allow people to drink all evening but still stay sober because every glass of wine is accompanied by a mouthful of tortilla or a salt cod croquette.**

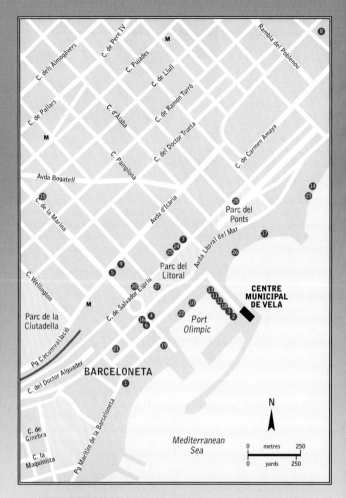

Port Olímpic

The Olympic Games of 1992 provided the impetus for a complete transformation of Barcelona's waterfront. One of the lasting legacies is the Olympic Village, a fashionable residential district which comes to life on summer weekends as the people of Barcelona head for the beaches and the restaurants which line the Olympic port.

Agua ❶

Passeig Marítim de la
Barceloneta 30

☎ 93 225 1272

Ⓜ Metro to Ciutadella-Vila
Olímpica

Open: Sun–Thu 1330–1630,
2030–2400, Fri–Sat 1330–
1620, 2030–0100

Reservations recommended

American Express

Seafood

❷❸

Situated right on the
beach beside the
Olympic port, this
restaurant attracts a
young and fashionable
crowd and is a great
place for an al fresco
meal. The menu features
classic seafood dishes
and rice cooked in a
coal fire, but there are
also modern
Mediterranean touches
such as cod cake with
sun-dried tomatoes.

El Cangrejo Loco ❷

Moll de Gregal 29

☎ 93 221 0533

Ⓜ Metro to Ciutadella-Vila
Olímpica

Open: daily 1300–0100

Reservations recommended

American Express

Seafood

❷❸❹

'The Crazy Crab' is one
of the best of the
seafood restaurants
around the harbour,
with tables overlooking
the beach and others
beside the port. You can
sit on the terrace
enjoying fresh seafood
tapas or go inside for a
more formal meal, based
around top-notch fish
dishes such as hake in
cider, monkfish casse-
role and salmon in
orange sauce.

El Celler del Rocxi ❸

Moll de Gregal 26

☎ 93 225 1965

Ⓜ Metro to Ciutadella-Vila
Olímpica

Open: Mon and Wed–Sat
1300–2400, Sun 1300–
1600

Reservations recommended

All credit cards accepted

Seafood

❶❷❸

There are so many fish
restaurants around the
port that it is hard to
know where to start, but
this is a good choice,
with unusual specialities
such as cod in three
cheeses and steak on a
hot tile. On Tuesdays,

▲ Agua

when this is closed, you can eat at the nearby **Rocxi Port** (closed Mon), which has the same owners and same menu.

Lungomare

C. de la Marina 16–18

✆ 93 221 0428

Ⓜ Metro to Ciutadella-Vila Olímpica

Open: Mon–Sat 1300–1600, 2030–2400, Sun 1300–1600

Reservations recommended

All credit cards accepted

Italian

Some of the best Italian cooking in Barcelona is found at the back of a skyscraper with views over the Olympic port. Start with grilled cockles in virgin olive oil, or a warm goats' cheese and vegetable tart, followed by fresh pasta with clams, hake and wild mushroom risotto, or roasted pigs' trotters with potato and cabbage pie.

La Marina

C. de la Marina 24

✆ 93 221 7702

Ⓜ Metro to Ciutadella-Vila Olímpica

Open: Mon–Sat 0800–2000

Reservations recommended

[VISA] [card]

Catalan

🄴

If you don't mind not being by the sea, this small restaurant on the edge of the Olympic Village offers a much better value alternative, with a daily lunch menu which might feature black rice or paella followed by a mixed grill of meat or fish. On the other hand, why come to this area at all if you don't want to eat lunch beside the sea?

Marina Moncho's

C. de la Marina 19

✆ 93 221 1514

Ⓜ Metro to Ciutadella-Vila Olímpica

Open: daily 1200–0200

Reservations recommended

All credit cards accepted

Seafood

🄴🄴

This is the seafront branch of a popular and reliable local chain of restaurants. Mussels are served in several styles with chips and garlic mayonnaise, or you can choose from ten different paellas (including vegetarian) or various fresh fish, such as sea bass, turbot or sole baked in the oven with a salt crust.

La Pegui

C. de Salvador Espriu 65–71

✆ 93 221 6643

🅜 Metro to Ciutadella-Vila Olímpica

Open: Tue–Sat 1300–1600, 2100–2400, Sun 1300–1600

Reservations recommended

💳 American Express

Brazilian

€€

Serious carnivores will enjoy the Brazilian meat buffet at this busy Olympic Village restaurant, where the meat comes cooked on skewers and you can eat as much as you like. Another speciality is *feijoada*, a hearty Brazilian casserole of *chorizo*, bacon and beans.

Els Pescadors ⑧

Pl. Prim 1

✆ 93 225 2018

🅜 Metro to Poble Nou

Open: daily 1300–1545, 2000–2400

Reservations essential

All credit cards accepted

Seafood

€€€

This popular restaurant is situated on an attractive old village square in the suburb of Poble Nou. It is known throughout Barcelona as one of the best places to eat seafood, especially in summer when there is a shady outdoor terrace. Most people opt for classic dishes such as paella, black rice, *fideuà* (noodle paella)

and oven-baked fish, but there are also some interesting vegetarian options. A little way off the beaten track, but it's well worth the detour.

El Racó de l'Havanera ⑨

Avda d'Icària 134

✆ 93 221 7193

🅜 Metro to Ciutadella-Vila Olímpica

Open: Mon 1300–1600, Tue–Sat 1300–1600, 2030–2300

Reservations recommended

All credit cards accepted

Catalan

€€

This lovely little cellar restaurant with exposed brick and wooden walls seems out of place in the ultra-modern Olympic Village. The cooking is traditional Catalan with a few inventive touches, such as salt cod with honey, monkfish carpaccio and grilled steak with roquefort sauce.

El Rey de la Gamba ⑩

Moll de Mestral 23–25

✆ 93 221 0012

🅜 Metro to Ciutadella-Vila Olímpica

Open: Tue–Sun 1200–2400

Reservations recommended

💳 💳

Seafood

€€

A tempting array of live lobsters and octopus is on display in tanks outside this restaurant, a branch of its bigger

namesake in Barceloneta. Prawns are the main attraction here, as the name implies, but you can also order oysters, clams, mussels, or a mixed grill of fish and seafood.

San Fermín ⑪

Moll de Gregal 22

✆ 93 221 0543

🅜 Metro to Ciutadella-Vila Olímpica

Open: Tue–Sun 1300–1600, 2000–2400

Reservations recommended

All credit cards accepted

Basque

€€

Amid all the near-identical seafood restaurants, this place stands out as it attempts to recreate the atmosphere of a Basque Country *sidreria*, a rustic cider barn where cider is poured from the barrel and huge steaks are cooked on an outdoor grill. You can even order the full *sidreria* menu, a Basque feast consisting of *chorizo* in cider, stuffed peppers, salt cod omelette, T-bone steak, cheese with walnuts and quince jelly, and all the cider you can drink.

La Taberna Gallega ⑫

Moll de Gregal 23

✆ 93 221 1524

🅜 Metro to Ciutadella-Vila Olímpica

Open: daily 1300–0100

Reservations recommended

▲ La Taberna Gallega

All credit cards accepted

Seafood

€€

The Galicians of north-west Spain are famed for their seafood, and this harbourside restaurant features the specialities of the region, as well as fishy *tapas* and some meat dishes. You can wash down your meal with a crisp Galician white wine.

El Tunel del Port ⑬

Moll de Gregal 12

☎ 93 221 0321

Ⓜ Metro to Ciutadella-Vila Olímpica

Open: Tue–Sat 1300–1600, 2030–2400, Sun 1300–1600

Reservations recommended

▭ ⬭ American Express

Seafood

€€€

Like most of the restaurants around the

Olympic port, this place is on two levels, with a summer terrace beside the harbour and a restaurant overlooking the beach. The menu features sophisticated fish dishes such as monkfish or grilled lobster with herbs, as well as venison fillet with apple marmalade. You can round off your meal with a truffle ice cream or lemon sorbet with vodka.

PORT OLÍMPIC
Bars, cafés and pubs

Catamaran

Platja de Bogatell

🚇 Metro to Ciutadella-Vila Olímpica or Llacuna

Open: Tue–Sun 1030–0100 in summer, Fri–Sun 1200–1600 in winter

All credit cards accepted

The last of the *chiringuitos* (beach bars) along Bogatell beach which are bringing back the atmosphere of pre-Olympic Barceloneta. You can eat a full meal in the restaurant or just sit on the terrace enjoying fishy *tapas* of steamed mussels, grilled prawns and fresh sardines.

Central Catalana del Pollastre ⑮

C. de Llull 32–38

🚇 Metro to Bogatell

Open: daily 1300–0100

All credit cards accepted

When you tire of designer chic around the port, seek out this barn in the back streets, offering roast chicken, chips, salad and sangría in the setting of a 19th-century warehouse. Children are made to feel welcome with a special menu and presents for those who finish their meal.

Flamenco & Son ⑯

C. de la Marina 19–21

🚇 Metro to Ciutadella-Vila Olímpica

Open: Tue–Sat 1300–1600, 2100–0300, Sun 1300–1630

Situated behind the **Hotel Arts** next to Frank Gehry's golden fish sculpture, this bar offers designer *tapas* such as duck breast with violet petals, duck liver in Cuban rum, and snails with ham and crystallised ginger. Come here late at night for cool music and a laid-back atmosphere.

Mango ⑰

Platja Nova Icària

🚇 Metro to Ciutadella-Vila Olímpica

Open: Mon–Thu 1000–1800, Fri–Sun 1000–0100 (daily 1000–0100 in summer)

🚇 American Express

This modern *chiringuito* or beach bar serves good, simple food at very reasonable prices. Come here for *tapas*, grills, cuttlefish and clam stew, or Catalan classics such as rice in fish stock with *allioli*.

Al Passatore ⑱

Moll de Gregal 25

🚇 Metro to Ciutadella-Vila Olímpica

Open: daily 1300–0100

One of the best places in the Port Olímpic for an informal and good-value meal, like its namesake in El Born (*see page 30*), it offers great Italian pizzas and fresh pasta dishes, but in an attractive waterfront setting.

Planet Hollywood ⑲

C. de la Marina 19–21

🚇 Metro to Ciutadella-Vila Olímpica

Open: daily 1300–0100

All credit cards accepted

▲ Mango

▲ *Chiringuito*

If you are tired of *tapas* and have a yearning for Caesar salad, burgers, chicken wings and other American fare, you know where to come. The advantage of this all-American themerie is that it has a terrace right on the beach.

Rincón del Jamón 🄴

C. de Salvador Espriu 23

🄼 Metro to Ciutadella-Vila Olímpica

Open: daily 0830–0200

VISA

The speciality of this traditional Catalan-style bar is ham, served with toasted tomato bread. The house special is a huge plate of charcuterie, designed for two to share. There is also a menu of *tapas* and grilled meat dishes.

Tapas Bar Marina Village 🄴

Avda Litoral del Mar 12–14

🄼 Metro to Ciutadella-Vila Olímpica

Open: Mon–Thu 0800–0100, Fri–Sat 0800–0300, Sun 1100–0100

All credit cards accepted

This branch of a successful *tapas* chain has plenty of seafood *tapas* and a good range of beers, wines and sherries, but the drawback is that it is situated just inland from the sea. If this was by the port with tables on the waterfront it would be every bit as popular as its counterpart at Port Vell (*see page 44*).

La Taverna del Cel Ros 🄴

Moll de Mestral 26

🄼 Metro to Ciutadella-Vila Olímpica

Open: Fri–Wed 1300–1700, 2000–2400

All credit cards accepted

Surrounded by fancier fish restaurants all around the port, this is more like an ordinary bar which happens to serve good fresh fish at decent prices. Among the house specialities are cod au gratin, seafood paella and sea bream baked with potatoes and onions.

Xiringuito Escribá 🄴

Platja de Bogatell

🄼 Metro to Ciutadella-Vila Olímpica or Llacuna

Open: Tue–Thu 1300–1600, Fri–Sun 1300–1600, 2100–2300 in winter; Tue–Sun 1100–0100 in summer

VISA

The people of Barcelona flock to this beach bar at weekends for fishy *tapas* such as minted sardines or octopus with potatoes, as well as simply grilled fish and classic rice dishes. As this is run by a famous family of pastry-makers, it also sells exquisite cakes for dessert.

PORT OLÍMPIC
Shops, markets and picnic sites

El Centre de la Vila ㉔

C. de Salvador Espriu 59

 Metro to Ciutadella-Vila Olímpica

Open: Mon–Sat 1000–2200

The 'centre of the village' is a faceless modern shopping mall designed to meet the needs of local residents and convince them that they are living in a real community. The Olympic Village has none of the charm of Barcelona's more traditional neighbourhoods, with their markets and family-run shops, and apart from a few newsagents and tobacconists, this is about all that there is. For everyday food shopping, there is a supermarket in the basement, along with a bakery, charcuterie, wine cellar, *tapas* bar, an ice cream parlour and various fast-food outlets. Not exactly La Boqueria market, but perhaps its late 20th-century equivalent. The only real reason for visiting is to stock up on goodies for a picnic by the beach.

Delicity ㉕

C. de Salvador Espriu 59

 Metro to Ciutadella-Vila Olímpica

Open: Mon–Sat 0800–2200, Sun 0800–1800

This café-deli in the 'main square' of Centre de la Vila sells homemade breads and pastries as well as cheeses, charcuterie and up-market picnic food ranging from luxury canapés to ready-prepared Catalan dishes such as baked salt cod. Outdoor tables in the square make it a pleasant place for a coffee and a cake in the sun.

Picnic sites

Beaches ㉖

 Metro to Ciutadella-Vila Olímpica

Although the restaurants of the Olympic port are one of the main attractions of this area, it is also a good place for a picnic and on summer afternoons half of Barcelona seems to be eating sandwiches on the beach. The beaches stretch away from the port in both directions, south towards Barceloneta and north alongside the Olympic Village.

Parc del Litoral ㉗

 Metro to Ciutadella-Vila Olímpica

Between the Olympic Village and the beach, Parc del Litoral is a pleasant green park, full of fountains, play areas and modern sculpture.

Parc del Ponts ㉘

 Metro to Ciutadella-Vila Olímpica

Parc del Litoral ends at Parc del Ponts, the 'Park with the Bridges', with grassy hills, wooden bridges and a rowing canal.

Late-night dining

Every night is a late night in Spain

For many visitors, every night is late night in Spain; after all, it is quite normal to sit down to dinner at 2200 or 2300. The fact is, though, that everything happens so late in Barcelona that after a few days this will not seem late at all. If you go to the theatre or the opera, you may not get out till midnight and you will be looking for somewhere to eat. And if clubbing is your scene, there is no point in starting before 0100 or 0200 so it makes sense to spend the early evening in bed and wander out for dinner at around midnight.

Most restaurants typically take their last orders sometime between 2300 and 2400, perhaps an hour or so later at weekends. Many bars, of course, stay open much later than this, and there is plenty of late-night action down by the waterfront and in places such as **Bar Ra**, **Mamacafé** and **Rita Blue** in El Raval (*see pages 12–13*). Old-style bars like **Café del Centre** and **Casa Alfonso** (*see page 62*) in L'Eixample can rustle up a snack late into the night. Of the restaurants featured elsewhere in this book, the following are open until at least 0100:

- **La Barbacoa de Gràcia** (*see page 79*)
- **Botafumeiro** (*see page 79*)
- **El Cangrejo Loco** (*see page 49*)
- **Marina Moncho's** (*see page 50*)
- **Al Passatore** (*see page 30*)
- **El Petit Miau** (*see page 41*)
- **El Pintor** (*see page 20*)
- **Pla de la Garsa** (*see page 30*)
- **Restaurant 7 Portes** (*see page 41*)
- **La Taberna del Cura** (*see page 81*).
- **La Taberna Gallega** (*see page 51*)
- **Tramonti 1980** (*see page 70*)
- **Travi Mar** (*see page 42*)
- **El Trobador** (*see page 71*)

Here are some further options for when those hunger pangs strike after midnight.

- **Asador del Mar** (*C. Borí i Fontestà 45; ✆ 93 201 2577; open: daily till 0100;* ❸❸❸) is an up-market roast house near **Turó Parc** which specialises in fish and seafood as well as red meat. This area is not served by the metro, so take a taxi.
- **Barceloneta** (*C. Escar 22; ✆ 93 221 2111;* Ⓜ *metro to Barceloneta; open: daily till 0100;* ❸❸❸) is a fashionable nautically themed seafood restaurant near the fishing port, with striped canvas tablecloths

▲ Restaurant 7 Portes

and picture windows overlooking the marina. As well as fresh seafood and paellas, it also offers a menu of grilled steaks.

• **Brasserie Flo** (*C. Jonqueres 10; ✆ 93 319 3102;* 🚇 *metro to Urquinaona; open: daily till 0100;* ❸❸❸) is a huge Parisian-style brasserie conveniently situated for musicians and concert-goers emerging from the nearby **Palau de la Música Catalana**. You are greeted in the porch by an enormous display of seafood, but the restaurant also features such French classics as duck breast and steak au poivre.

• **Café Salambo** (*C. Torrijos 51; ✆ 93 218 6966;* 🚇 *metro to Fontana; open: daily till 0230, meals till 0100;* ❸❸) in Gràcia is the favoured meeting-place of writers and artists after foreign-language films at the nearby Verdi cinema. The menu features moussaka, salads and carpaccio of salt cod, as well as vegetarian dishes.

• **Friends** (*C. Deu i Mata 125; ✆ 93 439 3556;* 🚇 *metro to Maria Cristina; open: Mon–Sat till 0100;* ❸❸❸) is a homely place in La Diagonal, with sofas, fireplaces and Eva Amber's personal style of cooking. There is no menu, it depends on what is in the market, but specialities include lentil casserole, cannelloni, paella and kid cooked in beer.

• **Giardinetto** (*C. Granada del Penedès 22; ✆ 93 218 7536;* 🚇 *FGC to Gràcia; open: Mon–Sat till 0130;* ❸❸) is a smart Italian restaurant off La Diagonal which has won awards for its interior design. The cooking is traditional, centred around homemade pasta, plus risottos, salads, carpaccios, grilled monkfish and tempting Italian desserts.

• **TNC** (*Pl. Arts 1; ✆ 93 306 5731* 🚇 *metro to Glòries; open: Tue–Sat till 0200;* ❸❸) is a restaurant inside the **Teatre Nacional de Catalunya**, a stunning modern theatre which opened in 1997 as the focal point of a new arts district. Come here after a show for Mediterranean cuisine, such as gazpacho, stuffed aubergines, pasta with scallops and fresh cheese with honey.

Except at weekends, the Metro system shuts down at 2300, so you will need to take a taxi to most of these places.

... the favoured meeting-place of writers and artists after foreign-language films at the nearby Verdi cinema ...

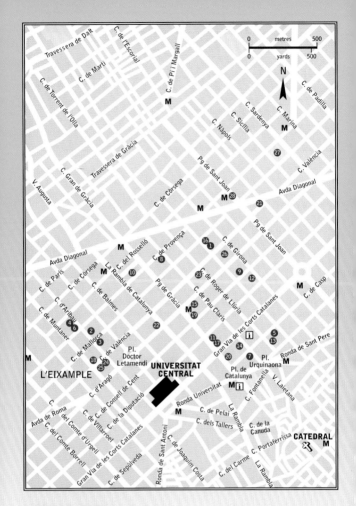

L'Eixample

The grid plan of L'Eixample ('extension') was devised in the 19th century to ease overcrowding in Barcelona. The main street, Passeig de Gràcia, is Barcelona's swankiest boulevard, lined with tapas bars and up-market boutiques, and the streets around here are home to some of the city's finest restaurants.

L'EIXAMPLE
Restaurants

Asador de Burgos ❶

C. dels Bruc 118

✆ 93 207 3160

🚇 Metro to Girona, Passeig de Gràcia or Verdaguer

Open: Mon–Sat 1300–1600, 2100–2300

Reservations essential

All credit cards accepted

Castilian

💲💲💲

This place is a vegetarian's nightmare, a Castilian-style roast house offering little other than meat, slow-cooked the proper way in a traditional tiled oven. You could start with a *cocido*, a hearty Castilian stew full of bacon, *chorizo* and pork fat, or a portion of lamb's liver or *morcilla* blood sausage. Follow this with roast piglet, roast lamb or a char-grilled veal steak. Salad? Only for wimps.

Bistrot 106 ❷

C. d'Aribau 106

✆ 93 453 2323

🚇 Metro to Hospital Clinic or FGC to Provença

Open: Mon–Fri 1300–1500, 2100–2330, Sat 2100–2330

Reservations recommended

💳 💳

French

💲💲

This intimate French bistro is *très Parisien*, with modern art on the walls, Piaf on the turntable and a menu featuring snails *bourguignonne*, beef *charolaise*, duck breast with figs and crêpes suzettes for dessert. Even the cheeses and wines are French.

Caballito Blanco ❸

C. de Mallorca 196

✆ 93 453 1033

🚇 Metro to Hospital Clinic or FGC to Provença

Open: Tue–Sat 1300–1630, 2045–2245, Sun 1300–1630

Reservations recommended

💳 💳 American Express

Catalan

💲💲

This well-known, traditional restaurant has starched white tablecloths, bow-tied waiters and formal Catalan-French cuisine. You could start with a selection of pâtés or charcuterie, followed by garlic prawns, sole meunière or a classic steak-*frites*.

La Camarga ❹

C. d'Aribau 117

✆ 93 323 6655

🚇 Metro to Hospital Clinic or FGC to Provença

Open: daily 1330–1530, 2100–2400

Reservations recommended

💳 American Express

Mediterranean

💲💲

This stylish modern restaurant is popular with businessmen for lunch and groups of friends at night. The speciality is rice, including risottos, paellas and *arròs caldoso*, a sort of rice soup in fish stock. More unusual dishes include carpaccio of ostrich, pigs' trotters with truffles and *trinxat de Cerdanya*, a Catalan version of bubble-and-squeak.

Casa Calvet ❺

C. de Casp 48

✆ 93 412 4012

🚇 Metro to Urquinaona

Open: Mon–Sat 1300–1600, 2100–2300

Reservations essential

All credit cards accepted

Mediterranean

💲💲💲

An up-market restaurant in the sumptuous Modernist setting of Antoni Gaudí's first apartment building in Barcelona. It offers refined versions of Catalan and Mediterranean cuisine, such as oyster ravioli in *cava*, partridge with chestnuts, and a mango and banana *tarte Tatin*.

Kowloon

C. d'Aribau 115

Ø 93 453 1753

🚇 Metro to Hospital Clinic
or FGC to Provença

Open: daily 1230–1600,
2000–2400

Reservations recommended

💳 💶

Chinese

💰💰

One of the top Chinese
restaurants in Spain was
the official base of the
Chinese delegation
during the 1992
Olympics. Among the
contemporary interpre-
tations of Chinese
cuisine are steamed
lobster with noodles,
Cantonese roast duck,
and sea bass with black
bean sauce.

La Maison du Languedoc-Roussillon ➐

C. de Pau Claris 77

Ø 93 301 0498

🚇 Metro to Urquinaona

Open: Mon–Fri 1330–1600,
2100–2300, Sat 2100–2300

Reservations essential

All credit cards accepted

French-Catalan

💰💰💰

This unusual place combines an art gallery, cultural centre, oyster shop and tourist office for 'French Catalonia' with a restaurant serving excellent southwest French cuisine. The favourites include *foie gras*, oysters, duck breast and beef in sweet Banyuls wines, accompanied by wines from the Roussillon, the region bordering Spain which historically formed part of Catalonia.

O'Nabo de Lugo

C. de Pau Claris 169
✆ 93 215 3047
🚇 Metro to Diagonal
Open: Mon–Sat 1300–1600, 2100–2400
Reservations recommended
All credit cards accepted
Seafood
💰💰💰

This top-notch *marisquería* features the seafood cookery of Galicia, based on simply prepared fresh ingredients. Good choices include sea bass baked in a salt crust, *kokotxas* (fritters of hake throat), and a selection of fried fish and shellfish. If you don't want the full works there are various lunchtime set menus, or you can just sit at the bar for a less formal meal of fishy *tapas* and shrimp *tortilla*.

El Rodizio ⑨

C. de Consell de Cent 403
✆ 93 265 5112
🚇 Metro to Girona
Open: Mon–Sat 1300–1600, 2030–2400, Sun 1300–1600
Reservations recommended
All credit cards accepted
Brazilian
💰💰

This popular Brazilian theme restaurant features an all-you-can-eat meat buffet as well as a carnival show with music and dancers on Thursday nights. Twelve different kinds of meat are available, from steaks to sausages, cooked on a spit and carved red-raw to your order. Children can eat for half price.

Tragaluz ⑩

Passatge de la Concepció 5
✆ 93 487 0621
🚇 Metro to Diagonal
Open: daily 1330–1600, 2030–2400
Reservations recommended
All credit cards accepted
Eclectic-Japanese
💰💰

Everyone who is anyone in Barcelona hangs out at this trendy restaurant, in a Renaissance palace given a makeover by design star Xavier Mariscal. The changing menu of fusion cooking emphasises fresh, simple ingredients, with several vegetarian and low-fat choices and a clear Japanese influence. During the evening the bar serves 'Japanese *tapas*' such as grilled Catalan sausage with cauliflower. The same owners have a Japanese sushi restaurant, **El Japonès**, across the street.

L'EIXAMPLE
Bars, cafés and pubs

Ba-ba-reeba 🄫

Passeig de Gràcia 28

🄫 Metro to Passeig de Gràcia

Open: daily 1230–0130

All credit cards accepted

One of several lively *tapas* bars with tables on the promenade, this also serves more substantial meals such as paella, grilled salmon and steak-*frites*, as well as *bruschetta* (toasted ciabatta bread) with various toppings.

Café del Centre 🄬

C. de Girona 69

🄫 Metro to Girona

Open: Mon–Sat 0700–0300

A famous old gaming hall and locals' bar with wooden tables and live piano music at weekends. The speciality here is the menu of *torrades*, which come on a wooden chopping-board with toppings ranging from Catalan sausage to Montsec goats' cheese and smoked duck breast to roasted vegetables.

Casa Alfonso 🄭

C. de Roger de Llúria 6

🄫 Metro to Urquinaona

Open: Mon–Tue 0900–2200, Wed–Fri 0900–0100

This classic local bar opened in 1934 and is now in the third generation of the same family. The simple menu focuses on sandwiches, cured ham and grilled meat dishes, along with exquisite pastries for dessert. A delicatessen at the front of the bar sells ham, sausages and cheeses.

Laie Llibreria Café 🄮

C. de Pau Claris 85

🄫 Metro to Urquinaona

Open: Mon–Fri 0900–0100, Sat 1000–0100

All credit cards accepted

Barcelona's original bookshop-café is a great meeting-place for young travellers, with tables outside in summer and live jazz on Tuesday nights. The menu is international, with several vegetarian choices such as spinach pancakes and vegetable risotto in addition to more traditional Catalan and Spanish fare.

Madrid-Barcelona 🄯

C. d'Aragó 282

🄫 Metro to Passeig de Gràcia

Open: Mon–Sat 1300–1530, 2030–2330

All credit cards accepted

You might have to queue at lunchtime to get into this popular bar, on the site of an old railway station on the Madrid-Barcelona line. There is a full menu of Catalan and Spanish dishes but most people seem to choose *pa amb tomàquet*, hunks of crusty tomato bread served with omelette, ham or crispy fried whitebait.

La Muscleria 🄰

C. de Mallorca 290

🄫 Metro to Girona or Verdaguer

Open: Mon–Fri 1300–1600, 2030–2400, Sat 2030–0100

The speciality here is mussels, steamed with roquefort, *allioli*, bechamel, *romesco* sauce or vinaigrette. The lunchtime formula of salad, mussels, chips, drink and ice cream is exceptional value.

Quasi Queviures 🄱

Passeig de Gràcia 24

🄫 Metro to Passeig de Gràcia

Open: daily 0800–0100

All credit cards accepted

'QuQu', as everyone calls it, is a delicatessen with a restaurant at the back and a *tapas* bar at the front offering a huge range of sandwiches and several unusual varieties of

Catalan sausage. Try the 'two flavour' toasts made with black and white pudding or smoked salmon and salt cod.

Taktika Berri [18]

C. de València 169

⊙ Metro to Hospital Clinic or Universitat

Open: Mon–Sat 1300–1600, 2030–2300

All credit cards accepted

This heaving Basque bar is busiest during the early evening when office workers stop off for a few *pintxos* on their way home. As well as the usual morsels of ham and cheese on pieces of bread, look out for warm snacks such as

stuffed hake or scrambled egg with wild mushrooms, washed down with Basque wine or cider.

Tapa Tapa [19]

Passeig de Gràcia 44

⊙ Metro to Passeig de Gràcia

Open: Mon–Sat 0730–0130, Sun 1100–0130

All credit cards accepted

It is bars like this that are responsible for the *tapas* vogue in Barcelona, with over 80 varieties of hot and cold *tapas* and outdoor tables on the sunny side of the street. Go with a friend and share a selection of snacks, such as shrimp croquettes, garlic

mushrooms and chicken in whisky.

Txapela [20]

Passeig de Gràcia 8–10

⊙ Metro to Catalunya or Passeig de Gràcia

Open: daily 1100–0100

All credit cards accepted

This is an attempt to take the Basque *pintxos* craze and turn it into an ordinary restaurant experience, with customers choosing from a picture menu rather than helping themselves from the bar. The food is authentic enough but it doesn't feel the same and takes away half the fun.

▲ Tapa Tapa

L'EIXAMPLE
Shops, markets and picnic sites

Shops

Almacen de Jamones Quesos y Embutidos ㉑

C. Roger de Flor

Ⓜ Metro to Verdaguer

Open: Mon–Sat 0900–1430, 1700–2100

VISA

If you're walking from the **Sagrada Família** towards Passeig de Gràcia, don't miss this extraordinary shop, with a huge selection of hams from all over Spain. There is Guijelo from Salamanca, Teruel from Aragón, and *jamón Ibérico de bellota*, produced in Extremadura from black pigs fed on acorns and known as the king of hams.

Colmado Quilez ㉒

La Rambla de Catalunya 63

Ⓜ Metro to Passeig de Gràcia

Open: Mon–Fri 0900–1400, 1630–2030, Sat 0900–1400

VISA ● American Express

The most famous grocer in Barcelona is a feast for all the senses, with bottles and cans piled floor to ceiling and an exceptional array of cheeses, cold meats and hams. Inside, the shop is bigger than it looks from the street and it is worth wandering into the wine cellar to explore the huge range of *cavas*, Catalan and Spanish wines.

Queviures Murrià ㉓

C. de Roger de Llúria 86

Ⓜ Metro to Passeig de Gràcia

Open: Mon–Sat 1000–1400, 1700–2100

VISA ● ⓓ

The most agreeably old-fashioned food shop in L'Eixample has become a Modernist landmark, with original tiled decoration and a shop front by Ramon Casas. Inside, you buy cheese, wine and coffee at separate counters and take your purchases to the cashier. There is a fine selection of cheeses from all over Spain and France, and

▲ Colmado Quilez

▲ Colmado Quilez

the wine cellar is pretty good too, including own-label *cava*. Ask for a card which lists the various Catalan wine regions and tells you which vintages to buy.

Reina ㉔

C. de València 202

🚇 Metro to Passeig de Gràcia or Universitat

Open: Mon–Sat 1000–2200, Sun 1000–1500

A high-class delicatessen and wine shop with a huge range of Riojas and *cavas* and a small wine-tasting *bodega* and sandwich bar at the back. As well as wine, the shop sells hams and charcuterie, cheeses, oils, vinegars and delicacies such as preserved peppers and asparagus from Navarra.

Xampany ㉕

C. de València 200

🚇 Metro to Passeig de Gràcia or Universitat

Open: Mon 1630–2100, Tue–Sat 1000–1400, 1630–2100

No credit cards accepted

The only shop in Barcelona totally devoted to *cava*, this is more like a museum than a shop, with dusty cabinets full of old champagne bottles, labels, corks and souvenirs. The owner certainly knows his *cava* and has more than a hundred types on display.

Markets

Mercat de la Concepció ㉖

C. de València

🚇 Metro to Girona

Open: Mon 0800–1500, Tue–Fri 0800–2000, Sat 0800–1600

This neighbourhood market somehow survives in the midst of busy, modern L'Eixample. It is based in a typical old iron-and-glass, art-deco market hall, with stalls selling meat, fish, fruit, bread and olives, but is best known for its fabulous flower displays, seen at the main

entrance on C. València. The little passages around the market are full of small shops and cafés, making this a pleasant area for escaping the bustle and noise of the surrounding streets.

Picnic sites

Passeig de Sant Joan ㉘

🚇 Metro to Verdaguer

Not far from the Sagrada Família, Passeig de Sant Joan has a green island with a children's play area close to Plaça Verdaguer – fine as long as you don't mind the noise of the traffic racing past on either side.

Sagrada Família ㉗

🚇 Metro to Sagrada Família

With its rigid street plan of identical square blocks, there is very little green space in L'Eixample and it is not the most obvious part of town for a picnic. The best bet is to head towards the Sagrada Família, Gaudí's unfinished cathedral and one of the highlights of any visit to Barcelona. The small parks to either side of the church are always crowded, but at least there is shade and the views make a great backdrop for a picnic.

Late-night bars

The art of drinking

The people of Barcelona like to go out, but on the whole they do not like to get drunk. Not in public, anyway. In fact, the Spanish are the biggest consumers of low-alcohol drinks in the world. Bars are places to meet up with friends, to talk politics or football, to listen to music while sipping a beer. The phenomenon of design bars which swept through Barcelona in the 1980s illustrates not just the city's obsession with style, but the fact that when you go out for a drink it is the experience that matters more than the drink itself.

Each district of Barcelona has its own bar culture. The waterfront areas of Port Vell and Port Olímpic are young and trendy, appealing mostly to foreign tourists.

El Born is fashionable too, but in a more sophisticated way. The designer bars are still found in L'Eixample, looking rather passé but worth a visit nonetheless,

▲ Café de l'Opéra

while El Raval shelters the remnants of the Barrio Chino, the red-light and music-hall district which has held so much fascination for visitors to Barcelona over the years.

All of the bars featured are essentially places for drinking, though some may have entertainment and/or food as well. Most of them are open from around 1900 in the evening, though this being Barcelona, the best time to go is after midnight.

LA RAMBLA AND EL RAVAL

During the day, **Café de l'Opéra** (*see page 12*) is an old-style coffee-house, but it is also lively late at night, when literary debates are held in the salon upstairs. Just up La Rambla, **Boadas** (*C. Tallers 1*) is a classy art-deco cocktail bar, opened in 1933 by a barman who learned his trade in Havana. This street leads off into El Raval, where lovers of low-life can make a late-night tour of the last vestiges of the Barrio Chino. **Marsella** (*C. Sant Pau 65*) is best known for its absinthe, a potent green liqueur with hallucinogenic qualities. **Bar Pastis** (*C. Santa Mònica 4*) is smaller and more intimate, a tobacco-stained bar opened in the 1940s by a Catalan artist returning from Marseilles. Bottles of Pernod line the shelves, Edith Piaf crackles out of the speakers and transvestite prostitutes tap on the windows as they walk past. Not far from here, **London Bar** (*C. Nou de la Rambla 34*) is an old-time music-hall pub with occasional cabaret shows. All of these places are safe to visit, but bear in mind that this is still a dodgy area late at night.

EL BORN

The late-night scene is mostly concentrated around the promenade of Passeig del Born, where Brazilian cocktail bars **Berimbau** (*No 17*) and **Miramelindo** (*No 15*) offer potent *mojitos, caipirinhas* and Latin jazz. Behind the promenade, **Pas del Born** (*C. Calders 8*) is a tiny back-street bar which is reviving the traditions of cabaret, with occasional variety shows and trapeze artists at midnight on Saturdays. For something more sophisticated, check out **Espai Barroc** (*C. Montcada 20*), a 'baroque space' in the courtyard of a 17th-century palace, with antique furniture, paintings and expensive fruit cocktails. Classical music concerts are held here at 1900 on Sundays, and there is opera by candlelight on Thursdays at 2300. Two places in this area to enjoy good wine and late-night snacks are **La Vinya del Senyor** and **Va de Vi** (*see page 34*).

L'EIXAMPLE

The design bars of L'Eixample date from the style-conscious 1980s, when hip designers such as Xavier Mariscal were running riot with post-Modern ideas like

factory furnishings and fluorescent toilets (for some reason, the toilets are always a feature of these bars, making you wonder just what you have been drinking). The original design bar is **Nick Havanna** (*C. Rosselló 208*), though others include **Velvet** (*C. Balmes 161*), with its red velvet curtains, and **Zsa Zsa** (*C. Rosselló 156*), where the walls are lined with Turkish rugs. **Snooker** (*C. Roger de Llúria 42*) doubles up as a bar and snooker club, with velvet banquettes, subdued lighting and a grand piano. Two unusual places in this district are **La Fira** (*C. Provença 171*), themed as a fairground with old dodgem cars and carousels, and **La Bolsa** (*C. Tuset 17*), 'The Stock Market', where the drink prices are displayed on a screen and fluctuate like shares according to demand. For more old-fashioned style, **Dry Martini** (*C. Aribau 166*) conjures up the atmosphere of 1930s Chicago, with white-jacketed waiters knocking up the best cocktails in town and an unmarked door giving it the appearance of a speakeasy.

> **When you go out for a drink it is the experience that matters more than the drink itself.**

La Diagonal

The broad sweep of Avinguda Diagonal cuts a swathe through L'Eixample, stubbornly defying the grid plan of the surrounding streets. West of Gràcia, this is Barcelona's central business district, home to offices, banks, department stores and the city's most exclusive restaurants and shops.

LA DIAGONAL
Restaurants

Altillo del Explorador ❶

Avda Diagonal 609–615

✆ 93 410 1317

🚇 Metro to Maria Cristina

Open: Mon–Sat 1300–1600, 2030–2400

Reservations recommended

VISA 💳 💳

Mediterranean

💶💶

Popular with the young executives who frequent this part of town, this grill restaurant over-looks the courtyard of the chic Pedralbes Centre shopping mall. The menu features fresh takes on traditional Catalan dishes, such as omelette with black truffles, pigs' trotters with mushrooms, and squid in its own ink with veal dumplings. Live piano music on Wednesday to Friday evenings.

L'Antull ❷

C. d'Europa 32

✆ 93 410 8929

🚇 Metro to Maria Cristina

Open: Mon–Sat 1300–1600, 2100–2300

Reservations unnecessary

All credit cards accepted

Catalan-Basque

💶💶

A short distance from the trendy spots of La Diagonal, this down-to-earth local restaurant offers seafood *tapas*, Basque cod dishes, grilled meats and other Catalan and Basque classics at sensible prices. In summer there are a handful of tables out of doors on a quiet street corner, so that you can sit and sun yourself.

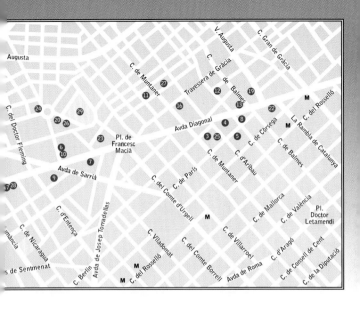

El Asador de Aranda ❸

C. de Londres 94

🕿 93 414 6790

🚇 Metro to Diagonal

Open: Mon–Sat 1300–1600, 2100–2300

Reservations recommended

All credit cards accepted

Castilian

❸❸❸

With tiled floors, long wooden tables and the constant aroma of wood smoke, this has all the character of a traditional Castilian roast house. The menu is composed almost entirely of meat dishes, notably roast lamb and suckling pig accompanied by serious red wines. Try to leave some room for the traditional Catalan and Spanish desserts.

La Dama ❹

Avda Diagonal 423

🕿 93 202 0686

🚇 Metro to Diagonal or FGC to Provença

Open: daily 1300–1530, 2030–2330

Reservations essential

All credit cards accepted

Catalan–French

❸❸❸

This formal restaurant in a sumptuous Modernist mansion is one of the best places in Barcelona for a really special night out. Among the highly personal interpretations of Catalan and French cuisine are salmon tartare, lobster paella, sea urchins in *cava* and sea bass with truffles and port. For the ultimate luxury, go for the *menu degustació*, a six-course gourmet menu.

Petit Paris ❺

C. de París 196

🕿 93 218 2678

🚇 Metro to Diagonal or FGC to Provença

Open: daily 1300–1600, 2100–2400

Reservations recommended

All credit cards accepted

Catalan–French

❸❸

This small, intimate bistro is a little bit of Paris in Barcelona,

▲ La Dama

offering refined versions of French and Catalan cuisine such as Provençal fish soup, lobster salad with mango, rice with Bresse pigeon, sole in *cava*, and beef with *foie gras*.

Satoru Miyano ⑥

C. de Ganduxer 18
✆ 93 414 3104
⒨ FGC to La Bonanova
Open: Mon 1330–1530, Tue–Sat 1330–1530, 2100–2330
Reservations recommended
All credit cards accepted
Japanese-French
€€€

Chef Satoru and his French wife Sophie create an unusual blend of Japanese and French cuisine at this stylish and sophisticated place behind Turó Parc. The starters are Japanese in tone, featuring sushi, *sashimi*, tuna tartare and lobster spring rolls, while the main courses have a Mediterranean feel and the desserts and pastries are purely French.

Tramonti 1980 ⑦

Avda Diagonal 501
✆ 93 410 1535
⒨ Bus to Pl. Francesc Macià
Open: daily 1300–1700, 2100–0100
Reservations recommended
All credit cards accepted
Italian
€€

Award-winning chef Franco Lombardo turns out some of the best Italian cooking in Barcelona. Try aubergine mousse or *bresaola* (air-dried beef), followed by lasagne or vegetable-stuffed *panze-rotti*, with homemade tiramisu or Italian ice cream to finish.

El Trobador ⑧

C. d'Enric Granados 122

✆ 93 416 0057

Ⓜ Metro to Diagonal

Open: daily 1230–0130

Reservations recommended

All credit cards accepted

Catalan

€€

With tables on the promenade and an open-plan tiled bar, this has become a popular place to meet. Grills are the speciality here, including meat (lamb chops, rabbit and sausages), fish and vegetables (mushrooms, asparagus and artichokes), though there are also daily specials and *tapas* which are served all day.

La Vaquería ⑨

C. Deu i Mata 141

✆ 93 419 0735

Ⓑ Bus to Pl. Francesc Macià

Open: Mon–Fri 1330–1600, 2100–2400, Sat 2100–2400

Reservations recommended

All credit cards accepted

Catalan

€€

Situated inside an old dairy, this is part restaurant, part piano-bar, part disco, attracting a mostly middle-aged crowd nostalgic for the 1980s. The food is simple and fresh, based on whatever is in the market, such as homemade hamburgers, steak tartare, seafood pancakes, salt cod dishes and duck breast in green peppercorn sauce.

Via Veneto ⑩

C. de Ganduxer 10

✆ 93 200 7024

Ⓕ FGC to La Bonanova

Open: Mon–Fri 1315–1615, 2045–2330, Sat 2045–2330

Reservations essential

All credit cards accepted

Catalan-French

€€€

One of the most famous restaurants in Barcelona combines exceptional service and first-class cuisine in an elegant Modernist setting. Among the expensive delights on offer are black truffles in *cava*, roast sole with banana, and a trio of steaks in different sauces. The desserts here are a treat, ranging from chocolate soufflé and rice pudding with coffee ice cream to more unusual choices such as banana ravioli or mango soup with fresh cheese.

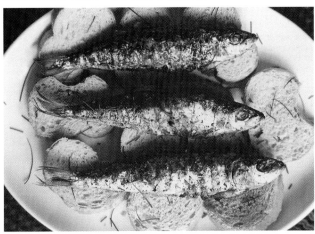

▲ Sardines

LA DIAGONAL
Bars, cafés and pubs

Casa Fernández ⓫

C. de Santaló 46

🚇 FGC to Muntaner

Open: daily 1300–0130

All credit cards accepted

This smart designer bar has a huge range of beers, both Spanish and imported, as well as a simple menu of *tapas*, salads, casseroles, burgers and pastries, available throughout the day. The house special is fried eggs with chips, which sounds unin-spiring but is offered in a dozen different styles.

Flash Flash ⓬

C. de la Granada del Penedès 25

🚇 FGC to Gràcia

Open: daily 1300–0100

All credit cards accepted

Once super-trendy and now retro-chic, Barcelona's original designer bar is stuck in the 1970s, with leatherette booths, formica tables and industrial white stools. More than 50 varieties of *tortilla* are on offer, along with simple snacks such as hamburgers and cheese puffs.

José Lluis ⓭

Avda Diagonal 520

🚇 Metro to Diagonal or FGC to Gràcia

Open: daily 0900–0100

All credit cards accepted

This well-known corner *tapas* bar makes a good place for lunch amid the chain stores and fashion emporia of La Diagonal. The main draw is the huge selection of *tapas*, mostly based on seafood and served both hot and cold.

Kitty O'Shea's ⓮

C. Nau Santa Maria 5

🚇 Metro to Maria Cristina

Open: daily 1200–0300

These days every city has its Irish theme pubs but this was the first in Barcelona, offering imported Guinness and whiskey, plus live sporting events on satellite TV. Food, such as smoked salmon and roast beef, is served on weekdays and also on Saturday evenings.

Mango ⓯

Avda Diagonal 635

🚇 Metro to Maria Cristina

Open: daily 0700–2400

💳 American Express

This is one of a number of restaurant-cafés with awnings out on the street in a bustling district of businessmen

and students. With cars rushing by this is not the best place for al fresco dining, but it's a good choice if you're in this area at lunchtime. The daily lunch specials are excellent value and there is a full menu of salads, grills, rice and pasta dishes and snacks.

Moncho's Barcelona ⓰

Travessera de Gràcia 44

🚇 FGC to Gràcia or Muntaner

Open: daily 1300–0100

All credit cards accepted

The flagship of the Moncho's empire which is rapidly expanding across Barcelona. Although this serves full meals including a buffet of grilled seafood and spit-roast meat, it is primarily a bar offering *tapas*, sandwiches and plates of ham and cheese to a young and lively crowd.

El Rincón del Jamón ⓱

L'Illa Diagonal, Avda Diagonal 557

🚇 Metro to Maria Cristina

Open: Mon–Sat 0900–2130

Despite its location inside the modern L'Illa shopping mall, this is actually an authentic *tapas* bar, with a good selection of *torrades* (toasts) served with ham and Catalan sausages. Hanging hams and strings of garlic are placed above the bar in conscious imitation of a traditional neighbourhood joint.

Si Señor

Avda Diagonal 593

Metro to Maria Cristina

Open: daily 1300–2400

American Express

'This restaurant does not appear in the Michelin guide', proclaims a sign outside this funky Mexican canteen, cocking a snook at the temples of gastronomy around it. Instead, it offers Tex-Mex dishes such as *fajitas*, tacos and chilli steak as well as fried fish in tequila.

Tapas Bar Via Augusta ⑲

Via Augusta 9

Metro to Diagonal

Open: Mon–Thu 0800–0100, Fri 0800–0200, Sat 1200–0200, Sun 1200–0100

All credit cards accepted

The popularity of *tapas* in Barcelona is largely down to this chain of bars which has brought a youthful, Mediterranean approach to this branch of Spanish cuisine. Come here for garlicky potatoes, spicy fried peppers, mussels, ham and cheese, accompanied by crusty tomato bread and a glass of sherry.

Tutusaus ⑳

C. Francesc Pérez Cabrero 5

Bus to Pl. Francesc Macià

Open: Mon–Fri 0900–2100, Sat 0900–1400

All credit cards accepted

The best cheese shop in town turns into a bar at lunchtime, with a simple menu based on the luxury products of the shop, such as smoked salmon, acorn-fed ham, caviar, *foie gras* and numerous varieties of cheese, all accompanied by homemade bread.

LA DIAGONAL
Shops, markets and picnic sites

Shops

El Corte Inglés ㉑

Avda Diagonal 617

🚇 Metro to Maria Cristina

Open: Mon–Sat 1000–2130

All credit cards accepted

Like its flagship branch in Plaça de Catalunya (*see page 14*), this well-known department store has a supermarket in the basement, and a gourmet delicatessen with charcuterie and cheese counters, chocolates and fresh-ground coffee, fresh fish, fruit and vegetables, a wine cellar and a sandwich bar. There is another La Diagonal branch at Plaça de Francesc Macià (*Avda Diagonal 471*).

Farga ㉒

Avda Diagonal 391

🚇 Metro to Diagonal

Open: daily 0800–2400

🏧 💳 American Express

This elegant patisserie sells superb chocolates and pastries and also has a delicatessen counter offering cheeses, *cava* and cured meats. The restaurant attached to the shop features refined versions of contemporary Catalan cuisine.

Jamón Jamón ㉓

C. del Mestre Nicolau 4

🚇 Bus to Pl. Francesc Macià

Open: daily 0900–0100

All credit cards accepted

Part *tapas* bar and part delicatessen, this place is a shrine to the Spanish worship of ham and other cured meats. Try some *jamón Ibérico de bellota* with a plate of *pa amb tomàquet* at the bar, then make your choice from a bewildering range of hams with names like Guijuelo, Jabugo, Huelva and Teruel.

Semon ㉔

C. de Ganduxer 31

🚇 FGC to La Bonanova

Open: Mon–Sat 0900–1400, 1600–2000, Sun 1000–1400

🏧 💳 American Express

This prestigious food shop is situated in the most up-market shopping district in town, catering for its well-heeled customers with such luxuries as Iranian caviar, home-produced *foie gras* and extra-virgin olive oil. There are also top-quality hams, sausages and cheeses, and a well-stocked wine cellar at the back of the store.

Torres Centre Cultural del Vi ㉕

C. d'Aribau 173

🚇 Metro to Diagonal

Open: Mon–Sat 1000–1400, 1630–2000

All credit cards accepted

Catalonia's best-known winemakers have opened a shop for the wine-lover, featuring wineglasses and decanters, corkscrews, wine books, everything to do with wine and of course lots of Torres wines from their estates

▲ Festival bread

in the Penedès vineyards.

Tutusaus 26

C. Francesc Pérez Cabrero 5

🚍 Bus to Pl. Francesc Macià

Open: Mon–Fri 0900–2100, Sat 0900–1400

All credit cards accepted

Surrounded by the designer boutiques on the edge of Turó Parc, Tutu's is the top cheese shop in Barcelona, featuring more than 40 varieties of Spanish cheeses including several from Catalonia, Mallorca and Menorca. It also specialises in French farmhouse cheeses, such as brie stuffed with truffles. Among the other gourmet foods on offer are smoked salmon, caviar with blinis and Iberian ham, all of which you can try in the attached *cava* bar.

Markets

El Rebost 28

L'Illa Diagonal, Avda Diagonal 557

🚇 Metro to Maria Cristina

Open: Mon–Sat 1000–2130

The basement of this huge modern shopping mall has been turned into a 'market', with stalls specialising in bread, ham, cheese, pasta, salt cod, fresh fish, meat, health foods, coffee, Catalan specialities and imported Italian products. At first sight it has little in common with Barcelona's more traditional neighbourhood markets but it is still a great place to buy picnic food. Instead of the workers' *tapas* bars found at markets like La Boqueria, this has espresso shops and wine bars reflecting its more up-market clientele.

Picnic sites

Turó Parc 29

🚍 Bus to Plaça Francesc Macià

Turó Parc is a small shady garden close to Plaça Francesc Macià at the heart of Barcelona's most exclusive shopping district. This is a great place to bring children on Sunday mornings, when puppet shows take place at an outdoor theatre in the park.

Kosher food 27

Barcelona's only kosher food shop is found close to the synagogue at C. Avenir 29 (open: Mon–Thu 1000–1300, 1530– 2000), serving the needs of the local Jewish community. Although this is essentially a butcher's shop, it also sells imported products such as kosher cheese from France and kosher wine from Israel. There are no kosher restaurants in Barcelona, though meals are served at the synagogue on Jewish holidays. Alternatively, see the feature on vegetarian restaurants (*see pages 86–7*).

Business dining

Impress your guest

The top business restaurants in Barcelona feature Catalan and French cuisine with Basque and Mediterranean influences. As with all Catalan cooking, the emphasis is on the quality of the ingredients but each chef will bring his or her own personal style. Most of these places are situated in the business areas of L'Eixample and La Diagonal, or further out in the suburbs, so it is best to take a taxi to reach them. The ambience at these restaurants is more formal than elsewhere, though none impose a strict dress code. Booking is essential, and most have private rooms available if booked in advance. All of the establishments below accept major credit cards, and except in the case of **Can Cortada** they come into the very expensive category – especially if you opt for the gastronomic menu and choose some good wines to accompany your meal.

Besides those restaurants listed here, the following are featured elsewhere in the book and would make suitable venues for a business meal:

- **Amaya** (*see page 9*)
- **Asador de Burgos** (*see page 59*)
- **Botafumeiro** (*see page 79*)
- **Ca L'Isidre** (*see page 9*)
- **Casa Calvet** (*see page 59*)
- **La Dama** (*see page 69*)
- **Jean Luc Figueras** (*see page 80*)
- **Passadís d'en Pep** (*see page 29*)
- **Restaurant 7 Portes** (*see page 41*)
- **Roig Robí** (*see page 80*)
- **Via Veneto** (*see page 71*).

- **Agut d'Avignon** (*C. Trinitat 3; ☏ 93 302 6034; ⊕ metro to Liceu*) is like a Catalan country house in the heart of the city, in a Barri Gòtic back-street close to the city hall. It offers fresh versions of traditional Catalan cuisine, along with hearty roasts and creations such as duck with figs. Even the King of Spain has eaten here.
- **El Asador de Aranda** (*Avda Tibidabo 31; ☏ 93 417 0115; ⊕ FGC to Avda Tibidabo; closed Sun eve*) is a roast house set in a Moorish-Modernist mansion on the tram route to Tibidabo. The speciality is roast lamb, eaten on the terrace in summer. In 1990 a male striptease artist was hired to entertain Madonna here.
- **Beltxenea** (*see page 17*) is a top-notch Basque restaurant, hidden away behind a discreet brass plaque on the first floor of a Modernist mansion. The tasting

RESTAURANT
Casa Calvet
1877

menu features creative versions of Basque seafood dishes. In summer you can eat out of doors on an interior garden patio.

• **Can Cortada** (*Avda L'Estatut de Catalunya;* ✆ 93 427 2315; Ⓜ *metro to Horta*) is situated in an 11th-century farmhouse, with a medieval atmosphere and a summer terrace beneath the hills. It features down-to-earth and very traditional Catalan cuisine, such as grilled meat, cod with spinach, chicken with crayfish and duck with pears, and of course *crema catalana* for dessert.

• **Can Travi Nou** (*C. Jorge Manrique;* ✆ 93 428 0301; Ⓜ *metro to Montbau; closed Sun eve*) is another farmhouse restaurant, offering refined Catalan-French cuisine in the splendid setting of an ivy-covered *masia*, with an outdoor terrace and several private banqueting rooms. The specialities include *foie gras* with calvados jelly and steamed langoustines with pigs' trotters.

• **Gaig** (*Passeig Maragall 402;* ✆ 93 429 1017; Ⓜ *metro to Horta; closed Sun eve and Mon*) began as a cart-drivers' café in 1869 and is still in the same family, offering sophisticated dishes such as pigeon with rice and wild mushrooms, turbot with goose barnacles, rack of lamb with juniper and homemade chocolate desserts.

• **Jaume de Provença** (*C. Provença 88;* ✆ 93 430 0029; Ⓜ *metro to Entença; closed Sun*

Roig Robí
Restaurant amb jardí

eve and Mon) is a small, exclusive restaurant in L'Eixample, where chef Jaume Barguès turns out exquisite Catalan dishes such as wild mushrooms with prawns and clams, or a mixture of pigs' trotters, truffles and *foie gras*.

• **Neichel** (*C. Beltrán i Rózpide 16;* ✆ 93 203 8408; Ⓜ *metro to Maria Cristina; closed Sat lunch and Sun*) is an elegant restaurant inside a modern apartment block in Pedralbes, where Alasatian chef Jean-Louis Neichel has gained two Michelin stars for his personal interpretations of such dishes as sole in Chardonnay and loin of lamb in an anchovy and herb crust. Cheeses, desserts and wines are superb, and there is a six-course truffle tasting menu for those whose budget will stretch that far.

> **It offers fresh versions of traditional Catalan cuisine, along with hearty roasts and creations such as duck with figs. Even the King of Spain has eaten here.**

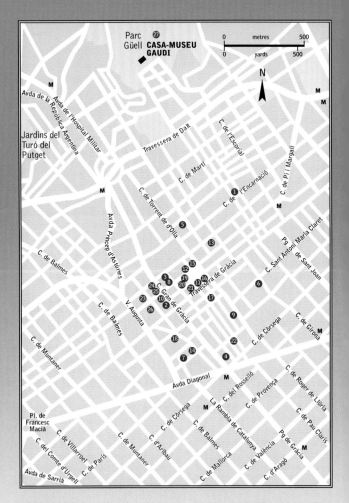

Gràcia

The former working-class township of Gràcia has a reputation for radicalism and a streak of independence which sets it apart. This individuality is reflected in the many restaurants and bars, which appeal to the local population of students and artists and make this an interesting area for a night out.

GRÀCIA
Restaurants

La Barbacoa de Gràcia ❶

C. Torrent Flores 65

☎ 93 210 2253

🚇 Metro to Joanic

Open: Wed–Sun 1300–1600, 2000–0100

Reservations recommended

[cards] 💳

Catalan

❷❷

This rustic-style grill with wooden tables and benches is bustling, noisy and authentically Catalan. Ignore the menu and ask what's on offer, or take a look at the meat in the chilled cabinet. You can start with toast, topped with anchovies, roasted vegetables or goats' cheese, but be warned that if you order the house special you will have no room left for the main course.

Botafumeiro ❷

C. Gran de Gràcia 81

☎ 93 218 4230

🚇 Metro to Fontana

Open: daily 1300–0100

Reservations essential

All credit cards accepted

Seafood

❸❸❸

Step inside this Modernist mansion with its polished wood furnishings for some of the finest seafood in Barcelona. The chef is from Galicia and the emphasis is on Galician fish dishes, such as sea bream and sea bass cooked on an open grill, along with fish soup,

lobster, black rice and seafood *fideuà*.

Ivan Rey ❸

C. del Montseny 10
✆ 93 218 2605
Ⓜ Metro to Fontana
Open: daily 1300–1600, 2000–2400
Reservations recommended
Catalan
❷❷

This popular back-street restaurant specialises in charcoal-grilled meat, including three different kinds of duck as well as steak, kid and snails with *allioli*. For a snack, try the platter of grilled vegetables, or the *surtido de torrades*, a selection of toasts topped with cheese, sausage, tuna and *escalivada* (roasted vegetable salad). Another speciality is scrambled eggs, cooked with prawns, salt cod or fresh garlic shoots.

Jean Luc Figueras ❹

C. Santa Teresa 10
✆ 93 415 2877
Ⓜ Metro to Diagonal
Open: Mon–Fri 1330–1530, 2030–2330, Sat 2030–2330
Reservations essential
American Express
French-Catalan
❸❸❸

The high priest of the new Catalan cuisine turns out elegant French-Catalan cooking in a neoclassical palace, with chandeliers and fine linen adding to the atmosphere of refined elegance. The emphasis is on seafood, game and offal, with unexpected combinations such as sea bream with *foie gras*, sea bass with Catalan sausage and salt cod tripe, or prawn salad with a summer cream of courgettes, ginger and orange. The chocolate desserts are to diet for.

Mesopotamia ❺

C. de Verdi 65
✆ 93 237 1563
Ⓜ Metro to Fontana
Open: Mon–Sat 2030–2345
Reservations recommended
▦ ●
Iraqi
❷❷

This trendy new restaurant, run by an Iraqi professor of languages, typifies the arty and cosmopolitan nature of this area. It serves contemporary Iraqi cuisine, such as aubergines in yoghurt, courgettes with mint, chicken with rosewater and cardamom, and homemade Mesopotamian bread.

Ot ❻

C. Torres 25
✆ 93 284 7752
Ⓜ Metro to Diagonal or Joanic
Open: Mon–Fri 1400–1530, 2100–2230, Sat 2100–2230
Reservations essential
▦ ●
Eclectic
❸❸❸

The hottest restaurant in town is run by two young chefs who provide a gastronomic experience for all the senses. There is no menu here, merely a set meal of eight courses which changes each month but might include such creative delights as monkfish, banana and bacon kebab or cream of artichoke with a lime and black pepper ice cream. Book well ahead.

Roig Robí ❼

C. de Sèneca 20
✆ 93 218 9222
Ⓜ Metro to Diagonal
Open: Mon–Fri 1330–1600, 2100–2330, Sat 2100–2330
Reservations essential
All credit cards accepted
Catalan
❸❸❸

Politicians and artists hang out at this elegant and formal back-street restaurant, which offers refined, modern versions of traditional Catalan cuisine. Among the options is a truffle tasting menu, featuring *foie gras* and truffle jelly, and truffle-stuffed squid. In summer you can eat out of doors on a pretty garden terrace.

Sho Jiro ❽

C. de Ros de Olano 11
✆ 93 415 6548
Ⓜ Metro to Fontana

Open: Mon 1330–1530,
Tue–Sat 1330–1530, 2100–
0030

Reservations recommended

VISA

Japanese

€€

This cool modern
restaurant blends
Japanese and
Mediterranean influ-
ences, featuring *sashimi*
of salmon, tuna and sea
bass and meat dishes
marinated in Japanese
sauces. Portions are
small but everything is
fresh and healthy, and
the daily-changing
lunch menu is always
good value. You can
round off your meal
with a chocolate or
apple tart.

Tábata 🟈

C. de Torrent de l'Olla 27

☎ 93 237 8496

🚇 Metro to Diagonal

Open: Mon 1300–1600,
Tue–Sat 1300–1600, 2100–
2400

Reservations recommended

All credit cards accepted

Catalan

€€

This fashionable
restaurant specialises in
meat and fish cooked on
tabas or slabs of hot
stone. It also features
large salads and
carpaccios of ostrich,
salmon, cod and veal, as
well as a vegetarian
menu of soup, salad and
dessert.

La Taberna del Cura 🔟

C. Gran de Gràcia 83

☎ 93 218 1799

🚇 Metro to Fontana

Open: daily 1300–0100

Reservations recommended

VISA American Express

Catalan

€€

This rustic tavern
attached to **Botafumeiro**
(*see page 79*) has
exposed brickwork and
hanging hams at the
bar. The speciality is
barbecued meat, with
chicken, lamb, rabbit,
sausages and steaks
cooked on an open grill
and a street stall selling
spit-roast chicken to
takeaway.

▲ Jean Luc Figueras

GRÀCIA
Bars, cafés and pubs

El 19 de la Riera 🄯

Riera de Sant Miguel 19

Ⓜ Metro to Diagonal

Open: Mon–Sat 1300–1600, 2000–2300

No credit cards accepted

This organic café is always busy at lunchtime, with a large salad buffet which is merely the first course in a good-value set meal. Although the food is mostly vegetarian, there are various organic meat dishes available for a supplement.

Amir de Nit 🄫

Pl. Sol 2

Ⓜ Metro to Fontana

Open: daily 1000–0100

💳 💳

This Lebanese café is a great place for coffee and Middle-Eastern sweetmeats on an open, sunny square. At meal-times it also functions as a restaurant, offering houmous, grilled meat, Lebanese bread and authentic dishes such as aubergines in sesame and pinenut sauce.

Café del Sol 🄬

Pl. Sol 16

Ⓜ Metro to Fontana

Open: Tue–Sun 1200–0200

No credit cards accepted

Gràcia is full of old-fashioned village squares where you can sit outdoors on summer evenings soaking up the unique atmosphere of this district. Plaça del Sol is the liveliest of all, lined with restaurants and bars, of which this is the most popular.

La Ceba 🄭

C. de la Perla 10

Ⓜ Metro to Fontana

Open: Mon–Sat 1300–1600, 2030–2400

No credit cards accepted

This bustling locals' bar specialises in *truita*, the Catalan version of *tortilla* or Spanish omelette. There are more than 50 varieties on offer, including courgette, aubergine and garlic shoots, as well as more traditional fillings.

Equinox Sol 🄯

Pl. Sol 14

Ⓜ Metro to Fontana

Open: daily 1300–0100

No credit cards accepted

This no-frills Lebanese takeaway claims to offer the best *falafel* in town, along with lamb,

▲ *Tapas*

chicken and houmous in pitta bread. It is cheap and cheerful, but very popular, with tables outdoors on a lively square.

Lizarran 16

Travessera de Gràcia 155
◉ Metro to Fontana
Open: daily 0900–2400
All credit cards accepted

This branch of a popular Basque *tapas* chain is the best place in Gràcia to try the titbits known as *pintxos*. These morsels of ham, cheese or fish on pieces of bread are available throughout the day, but the busiest time is during the early-evening *txikiteo*, when groups of friends wander from bar to bar drinking small glasses of Basque cider and fizzy *txakoli* wine.

Nou Candanchú 17

Pl. Rius i Taulet 9
◉ Metro to Fontana
Open: daily 0900–0100
🖃 🍴

This café in the corner of one of Gràcia's largest squares is a good place to sit out of doors beneath the clock tower in summer. It serves *tapas*, omelettes, sandwiches, paella and grilled meat and fish dishes, but its essential appeal is as an enjoyable pavement café.

El Roble 18

C. Lluís Antúnez 7
◉ Metro to Diagonal or Fontana
Open: Mon–Sat 0700–0100
No credit cards accepted

This is what *tapas* bars used to be like before the arrival of designer tapas in Barcelona. A bustling back-street bar, always busy, where the locals gather to smoke and drink beer while tucking into generous portions of mussels, anchovies, meatballs and cured ham.

Sol Solet 19

Pl. Sol 13
◉ Metro to Fontana

Open: Mon–Fri 1800–0130, Sat–Sun 1800–0230
No credit cards accepted

This unusual bar features wholefood *tapas*, such as couscous, Greek salad, quiches, sesame prawns and herby wholemeal tomato bread, as well as delicious cakes and pastries. The best thing to do is to go here in a group and order lots of dishes to share.

Tetería Jazmín 20

C. Maspons 11
◉ Metro to Fontana
Open: Tue–Sun 1800–0200
No credit cards accepted

This cool Moroccan tea-room makes a great place to wind up after a night-time bar crawl through this district. With hanging carpets, sofas, low stools and mint tea in copper pots, it has all the flavour of Marrakech. The tea comes with dainty Arabic sweetmeats, or you can order a vegetarian couscous.

GRÀCIA
Shops, markets and picnic sites

Shops

La Botiga del Sol 21

C. Xiquets de Valls 9

🚇 Metro to Fontana

Open: Mon–Fri 1000–1400, 1700–2000, Sat 1000–1400

No credit cards accepted

Situated in the heart of alternative Gràcia on the corner of its liveliest square, this wholefood shop features an impressive range of bread, pasta, dried fruit and nuts plus organic fruit and vegetables, cheese and yoghurt, ready-to-eat pasties and serious dark chocolate.

Especialidad en Jamones Serranos de Salamanca y Teruel 22

C. Bonavista 24

🚇 Metro to Diagonal

Open: Mon–Sat 0800–1430, 1700–2030

No credit cards accepted

The name of this shop says it all, and if you don't understand the name you only have to look at the haunches of ham which hang around the walls. If you are after a whole ham to take home, this unpretentious back-street shop is a lot cheaper than the better-known places, and also sells *chorizo*, Catalan sausages and Manchego sheeps' cheese.

Ponsa 23

C. de Berga 3

🚇 Metro to Fontana

Open: Mon–Fri 1000–1400, 1700–2000, Sat 1000–1400

No credit cards accepted

This small shop beside the market opened in 1952 and specialises in pre-cooked vegetables, including lentils, chickpeas, spinach and beans, displayed in buckets and sold by weight. Cooked pasta and rice are also available, so you have all the ingredients you need for a healthy vegetarian salad.

Sicart 24

C. Gran de Gràcia 111

🚇 Metro to Fontana

Open: Mon–Sat 0800–1430, 1700–2030

This top-notch delicatessen on Gràcia's main street sells homemade *chorizo* sausages as well as mountain hams and Pyrenean cheeses. Among the other items on display are pâtés and mousses, ready-prepared dishes, *cava*, wine, olive oil and sherry vinegar.

Xarcuters 25

C. Gran de Gràcia 93

🚇 Metro to Fontana

Open: Mon–Sat 0830–1400, 1700–2030

This place, with huge hams hanging down from the ceiling and an entire *jamón Ibérico de bellota* on display in the window. If you don't want to buy a whole ham, you can have some slices carved for you, or choose from the impressive array of charcuterie, cheeses and wines.

▲ Park Güell

Markets

Mercat de la Llibertat 26

Pl. Llibertat

◉ Metro to Fontana

Open: Mon–Sat 0800–1400, 1700–2000

This magnificent Modernist market hall, designed by a pupil of Antoni Gaudí, is where the locals come to shop. The independent spirit of Gràcia is reflected in its name, which means 'freedom'. The market has a busy, small-town feel, with stalls selling meat, fish, cheeses and fresh produce as well as several specialising in wholefoods, such as pistachios, almonds, dried apricots, figs and honey. The streets around the market are full of ordinary food shops which have a real buzz during the morning. Don't miss the *huevería* on the north side of the square, which sells nothing but eggs.

Picnic sites

Park Güell 27

◉ Metro to Vallcarca or bus 24

This unfinished garden city designed by the Modernist architect **Antoni Gaudí** is one of the most enjoyable places in Barcelona. Children love the fantasy architecture, with fairy-tale gatehouses and a dragon stairway, while adults enjoy strolling high above Barcelona with views down over the city. At the centre of the park is an esplanade, designed as a town square and surrounded by an undulating park bench created out of *trencadís* or broken ceramics. Not far from here, the house where Gaudí spent the last years of his life has been converted into a museum. It takes around 30 minutes to walk to the park from Gràcia, but it is a stiff hike and a steep climb. It is better to save your energy and take the Metro two stops from Fontana to Vallcarca. Just south of Vallcarca station, Baixada de la Glòria leads up to the park, with outdoor escalators which save your legs and add to the sense of fun. Alternatively, take bus no 24 from Gràcia direct to the park entrance.

Vegetarian restaurants

An emerging cuisine

You might be forgiven for thinking that a country whose delicacies include pigs' trotters and salt cod tripe would not exactly be friendly for vegetarians, and in a sense you would be right. Traditionally, vegetarians have had a hard time in Barcelona, forced to endure endless potato omelettes and salads which claimed to be vegetarian but turned up with pieces of tuna or blood sausage on the plate. Finally, though, things are looking up. The large population of foreign students, combined with the city's cosmopolitanism and a new opening to outside influences, means that vegetarianism has arrived in Barcelona. There are now more than 40 vegetarian restaurants in the city, almost as many as in the whole of the rest of Spain. Even better, those restaurants which serve meat and fish are also starting to offer truly vegetarian options, particularly the trendier

establishments in youthful parts of town such as Gràcia, El Raval and El Born. The slow move away from traditional Catalan cooking towards a more eclectic, international style has certainly been good news for vegetarians.

EL RAVAL

There are two good options in the northern half of El Raval, close to the contemporary art museum. **L'Hortet** (*see page 11*) is the more appealing, but **Biocenter** (*C. Pintor Fortuny 25; ∅ 93 301 4583;* ⊕ *metro to Liceu; open: Mon–Sat 0900–1700; no credit cards accepted;* ❶) is better established, offering salads, omelettes and a four-course lunch menu, with an organic and health food shop across the road. Around the corner, **Mamacafé** (*see page 13*) is a funky bistro with several vegetarian choices, and the Pakistani restaurants scattered throughout this district also make a good choice for a vegetarian meal.

BARRI GÒTIC

Govinda (*Pl. Vila de Madrid 4; ∅ 93 318 7729;* ⊕ *metro to Catalunya; closed Sun and Mon evening;* ❶❶) is an old-fashioned Indian standby, offering mild curries, lentil soup and vegetarian *thalis* (mixed plates), as well as European dishes such as pizzas and pancakes. There is no alcohol but you can accompany your

meal with lime-flavoured *lassi* or spicy Indian tea. Another well-established place is **Self Naturista** (*C. Santa Anna; ✆ 93 318 2388;* **⦿** *metro to Catalunya; closed Sun; no credit cards accepted;* **❶**), a self-service canteen offering soups, stews and salads. The food is fine but the atmosphere conveys the out-of-date message that vegetarian cookery is worthy but dull. By contrast, **Juicy Jones** (*C. Cardenal Casañas 7; ✆ 93 302 4330;* **⦿** *metro to Liceu; open: Tue–Sun 1300–2300; no credit cards accepted;* **❶**) is a wacky vegetarian juice bar, with brightly painted murals and hippy slogans such as 'Life is Beautiful' and 'Smile to the World'. You can drop in at any time for a freshly squeezed fruit and vegetable juice, but there is also an excellent set lunch menu of soup, a hot dish of the day with salad and a juicy dessert.

❶), a huge wholefood complex with a snack bar, self-service buffet, food shop and a restaurant serving pizzas, pasta dishes, salads, tofu and spring rolls.

GRÀCIA

With its large student population and its reputation for alternative lifestyles, Gràcia is an obvious area for vegetarians and the cafés around Plaça del Sol make a good start, especially **Sol Solet** (*see page 83*) with its wholefood *tapas*.

> ... a wacky vegetarian juice bar, with brightly painted murals and hippy slogans such as 'Life is Beautiful' and 'Smile to the World' ...

EL BORN

Although it is not exclusively a vegetarian restaurant, the best choice in this area has to be **La Flauta Mágica** (*see page 29*), whose New Age cuisine has taken vegetarian cookery on to a different plane with dishes such as rose-petal omelette, banana leaves stuffed with jasmine rice, and mango and vegetable brick with curry sauce. For more conventional vegetarian fare, head for **Comme–Bio** (*V. Laietana 28; ✆ 93 319 8968;* **⦿** *metro to Jaume I; open: Mon–Sat 0800–2330, Sun 1200–2330;*

Two other places in this area are **La Buena Tierra** (*C. Encarnació 56; ✆ 93 219 8213;* **⦿** *metro to Joanic; closed Sun;* **❶**), more like a private house with tiled floors and a pretty garden terrace, which does an excellent four-course vegetarian lunch, and **L'Illa de Gràcia** (*C. Sant Domenec 19; ✆ 93 238 0229;* **⦿** *metro to Fontana; closed Mon;* **❶**), a trendy vegetarian restaurant with a varied menu of salads, pancakes, pasta dishes, omelettes, tofu burgers and homemade ice cream.

Food etiquette and culture

Food and drink are central to the Catalan way of life. Friendships, business deals, family life and celebrations all revolve around the table. Here, food is not merely something to be eaten, but something to be savoured and enjoyed, preferably at length.

MEALTIMES

Some foreigners find it difficult to adjust to the rhythm of the Spanish day. Compared with the rest of Europe, everything happens very late. Breakfast might be a coffee and a pastry or a sandwich and a beer, taken at any time up to about 1200. For most people, the main meal of the day is lunch, which generally begins around 1400 and never before 1300. Dinner is taken from around 2100, though it may be as late as 2300. Fortunately, the Spanish have found a way of filling the gaps. Between 1900 and 2100 each night, you will see groups of friends hopping from bar to bar nibbling on snacks before going home for a proper meal.

RESTAURANTS
The different menus
The basic choice at most restaurants is between the *menú del día* (set menu) and the *carta* (à la carte). Almost all restaurants offer a *menú del día* at lunchtime and some in the evening too. This is a set meal, usually of three courses, with house wine or water included, and will always be much cheaper than if you had ordered the same dishes from the *carta*. The choice may be limited to two or three items for each course, but the food will be fresh and filling, and this usually represents a good deal. You might start with paella, soup or salad, followed by grilled meat or fish with chips. Other vegetables will be notable by their absence. Desserts are usually uninspired, perhaps fruit, *flan* (crème caramel) or ice cream, but if you are lucky you may be offered *crema catalana* (Catalan burnt custard). The wine will be drinkable, but you will notice that some people choose to add water or lemonade to theirs.

Obviously, if you go for the *carta*, you have a wider choice and can expect the food to be more refined. You may even find that the waiter brings you a new knife and fork between courses. Don't worry about choosing the right wine with your meal. The Catalans are refreshingly unfussy about wine, and though they certainly enjoy a good wine there is little snobbery involved. In fact you will notice that they usually drink red, even with fish, or perhaps a light rosé in summer. The house wine will probably be

Catalan and is usually quite acceptable. If you don't want to drink alcohol, mineral water makes a good alternative.

MANNERS
The Spanish eat for pleasure and there are few rules of etiquette to be observed. If you are choosing from the *carta*, feel free to ask for two starters, or one main course for two people to share. Children are welcome in all but the smartest establishments, and there are very few places where you need to dress up. One aspect of this informality which may not appeal to everyone is that, with few exceptions, smoking in restaurants is quite normal and acceptable.

RESERVATIONS
It is always a good idea to book a table in advance on Friday and Saturday nights and for Sunday lunch. Many restaurants are closed on Sunday evenings, and some on Mondays as well. A number of restaurants close for an annual holiday, usually in August.

BARS
Tapas
The *tapas* bar (*see pages 46–7*) is a Spanish institution. In traditional stand-up bars, the snacks are displayed beneath the counter and you simply point to what you want or choose from a blackboard menu. A *tapa* is a small portion, a *ración* is larger, but remember that *tapas* are not supposed to be a substitute for a meal. Order enough of them, though, and it can easily turn into a meal. Another way of filling up is to graze on *pintxos*, those bite-sized Basque snacks which are featured in numerous bars, especially in El Born. The etiquette here is to ask the barman for a plate, help yourself from the bar, keep your cocktail sticks and count up how many you have had when the time comes to pay the bill. As in all bars, it is customary to leave some small change on the counter when you go.

Bar food
Most bars offer snacks at any time of day from breakfast to late at night. You will almost always be able to get a *bocadillo* (filled roll) or a plate of *pan con tomate* with ham or cheese. Many bars offer a much fuller menu, including *platos combinados* (combined plates) such as fried eggs, hamburger, salad and chips.

TIPPING
By law, restaurant bills must include a service charge but it is customary to leave a small extra tip of around 5 per cent.

Menu decoder

A NOTE ABOUT LANGUAGE

Most restaurant menus in Barcelona are printed in both Catalan and Spanish, and many have English translations as well. The list below includes both Catalan and Spanish terms, though mostly Spanish, depending on what you are most likely to see on the menu.

CATALAN SPECIALITIES

The following dishes are Catalan specialities which invariably appear in Catalan. They might be accompanied by *allioli* (garlic mayonnaise) or *romesco* (a sauce of hazelnuts, almonds, tomatoes, garlic and olive oil).

amanida catalana – large mixed salad of fresh and pickled vegetables, topped with olives, hard-boiled egg, tuna, anchovies and cold meats

ànec amb peres – stewed duck with pears

bacallà a la llauna – baked salt cod with garlic, tomatoes and white wine

botifarra amb mongetes – grilled Catalan sausage with white beans

calçots a la brasa – barbecued spring onions with *romesco* sauce (*see page 26*)

cargols a la llauna – baked snails with *allioli*

espinacs a la catalana – spinach with pinenuts and raisins

faves a la catalana – stewed broad beans with blood sausage and pork

oca amb naps – casserole of goose with turnips

peus de porc – pigs' trotters

pollastre amb samfaina – roast chicken with Catalan ratatouille

sípia amb mandonguilles – cuttlefish with meatballs

suquet de peix – casserole of assorted white fish with potatoes, tomatoes and white wine

TAPAS

The following are the Spanish terms for the most common *tapas* dishes, which can be ordered as *tapas* (small portions) or *raciones* (larger helpings). All of them can be accompanied by *pan con tomate*, or *pa amb tomàquet* in Catalan (*see page 27*).

albondigas – meatballs in tomato sauce

boquerones – fresh anchovies marinated in wine vinegar

calamares a la romana – battered fried squid rings

chorizo al vino – spicy pork sausage in red wine

croquetas – deep-fried croquettes, filled with minced meat, salt cod or ham and cheese

ensaladilla rusa – 'Russian salad', or cold potatoes and vegetables in mayonnaise

gambas al ajillo – garlic prawns

jamón serrano – cured mountain ham – the best-known is *jamón Ibérico de bellota*, derived from acorn-fed black pigs

mejillones al horno – baked mussels

patatas allioli – potatoes in garlic mayonnaise

patatas bravas – potatoes in a spicy tomato sauce

pimientos de padrón – deep-fried green spicy peppers from Galicia

pulpo gallego – boiled octopus with paprika and olive oil

tortilla española – the classic Spanish omelette, more like an egg and potato cake, served warm or cold with bread

SOUPS, SALADS AND STARTERS

ajo blanco – chilled summer soup of almonds, garlic and grapes

alcachofas con jamón – sautéed artichokes with pieces of cured ham

berenjenas rellenas – aubergines stuffed with minced beef

entremeses – a selection of hors d'oeuvres, usually including cured ham as well as sausages such as *chorizo, fuet* (Catalan salami) and *morcilla de Burgos* (blood sausage)

escalivada – a Catalan salad of roasted aubergines, peppers and onions in olive oil

esqueixada – Catalan salad of raw, shredded salt cod with tomatoes, onions and olives

gazpacho andaluz – the classic summer soup, a chilled and blended salad of bread, tomatoes, garlic, peppers, olive oil and vinegar

judías verdes con jamón – green beans sautéed with pieces of cured ham

menestra de verduras – sautéed vegetables – vegetarians should be aware that ham is sometimes added for flavour, and that meat stock is often used

patatas a la riojana – potatoes with red peppers and *chorizo* sausage

pimientos rellenos – peppers stuffed with pork or salt cod

revuelto de ajos tiernos – scrambled eggs with garlic shoots – alternatives are *revuelto de setas* (wild mushrooms) or *espárragos* (asparagus)

sopa de ajo – garlic soup, thickened with bread and egg

xató – Catalan spring salad of salt cod, tuna, anchovies and lettuce with a *romesco* dressing

RICE DISHES

Rice dishes such as paella are given a separate section on the menu. Unless it is pre-cooked as part of a *menú del día*, a good paella takes at least 20 minutes to produce and the effort involved means that it is usually only available for a minimum of two people.

arròs negre – the Catalan equivalent of paella is known as 'black rice', blackened by the ink of the cuttlefish which are included along with other seafood

arroz caldoso – a rice and fish broth, known as the poor man's paella

fideuà – not strictly a rice dish but usually grouped with them on the menu, this is a seafood paella made with vermicelli noodles instead of rice

paella de mariscos – seafood paella

paella parellada – 'blind man's paella', served without bones

paella valenciana – the original paella, of saffron rice with chicken, rabbit, green beans, peppers and usually, though not invariably, seafood

FISH DISHES

The best fish and seafood dishes are often the simplest, such as grilled *lenguado* (sole) or *parrillada de mariscos*, a mixed seafood grill. Among the fresh fish and shellfish which you are likely to see on the menu are *almejas* (clams), *besugo* (sea bream), *calamares* (squid), *cigalas* (crayfish), *gambas* (prawns), *langosta* (spiny lobster), *langostinos* (langoustines), *lubina* (sea bass), *mejillones* (mussels), *merluza* (hake), *pulpo* (octopus), *rape* (monkfish), *salmón* (salmon) and *sepia* (cuttlefish).

bacalao a la vizcaina – a Basque dish of salt cod with peppers and sweet chillies

bacalao pil-pil – casserole of salt cod in a light garlic sauce, also a speciality of the Basque Country

lubina a la sal – sea bass baked in a salt crust

merluza a la vasca – a Basque dish of hake in a white wine sauce

merluza en salsa verde – hake in a parsley sauce, usually with other seafood

zarzuela – seafood 'operetta', known as *sarsuela* in Catalan (*see page 94*)

MEAT DISHES

As with fish, the Catalan way with meat is to cook it simply, and some of the best restaurants are those which offer *carnes a la brasa* (charcoal-grilled meat). Another alternative is the *asador*, a Castilian-style roast house where meats such as lamb and suckling pig are slow-roasted in a traditional brick oven. Among the most common meats are *buey* (beef), *cabrito* (kid goat), *cerdo* (pork), *conejo* (rabbit), *cordero* (lamb), *pato* (duck), *pollo* (chicken) and *ternera* (veal).

chuleton de buey – enormous T-bone steak, a speciality of the Basque Country

civet de jabalí – wild boar casserole, a popular winter dish in the Catalan Pyrenees

cochinillo asado – tender, slow-roasted suckling pig

cocido castellano – Spain's national dish is a thick stew of pork, chicken, *chorizo*, ham, potatoes, cabbage, chickpeas and much more, usually served over two or

three courses

conejo al ajillo – rabbit in garlic, or with *allioli* (garlic mayonnaise)

cordero asado – slow-roasted lamb – the best is milk-fed lamb less than a month old

entrecot a la brasa – chargrilled entrecôte steak, sometimes served with a peppercorn or blue cheese sauce

fabada asturiana – the Asturian equivalent of a *cocido*, a thick stew of salt pork, blood sausage, *chorizo*, saffron and white beans

magret de pato – duck breast, usually grilled and served in thin slices but occasionally whole, known as *magret d'ànec* in Catalan

pollo al ajillo – garlic chicken

pollo al chilindrón – chicken in a tomato, pepper and onion sauce, a speciality of Aragón which is similar to the Catalan dish *pollastre amb samfaina* (see page 90)

DESSERTS

Desserts are not Spain's strong point, and in many places you will simply be offered a choice between fruit and *helado* (ice cream), but you may also see some of the following:

arroz con leche – cold rice pudding, flavoured with cinnamon

crema catalana – Catalan burnt custard (see page 94)

cuajada – similar to a yoghurt, but in fact a milk junket, served in earthenware pots and best eaten with honey

flan – crème caramel

mel i mató – a Catalan speciality of curd cheese with honey – the Spanish equivalent is *requesón con miel*

DRINKS

agua mineral – mineral water (*con gas* – sparkling, *sin gas* – still)

café con leche – coffee with hot milk

café cortado – espresso coffee with a dash of hot milk

café solo – small, black espresso coffee

cava – Catalan sparkling wine, similar to champagne

gaseosa – any fizzy drink, usually soda water or lemonade

manzanilla – camomile tea, or a very dry sherry

sangría – chilled summer punch of red wine, fruit and lemonade, sometimes with brandy added

txakoli – a slightly fizzy, tart white wine from the Basque Country

vino blanco – white wine (*vi blanc* in Catalan)

vino rosado – rosé wine (*vi rosat* in Catalan)

vino tinto – red wine (*vi negre* in Catalan)

zumo de naranja – orange juice

Recipes

Sarsuela de peix (Seafood operetta)

This popular dish was invented in the seafood restaurants of Barceloneta in the late 19th century. Its name (zarzuela in Spanish) means a light operetta or musical comedy, the idea being that this is a fun dish with a little bit of everything thrown in. There are as many recipes for sarsuela as there are Catalan chefs, but all have in common an abundance of fish and seafood, cooked in a white wine and saffron broth. You can vary the fish and shellfish to suit your taste and budget, or whatever is in the market.

Serves 4

INGREDIENTS

1kg white fish, such as fillets of hake, grouper, monkfish, or sea bass

1 large squid

4 large prawns

250g mussels

200g clams

2 large onions, chopped

3 medium tomatoes, peeled, seeded and chopped

white wine

1 litre fish stock

saffron

garlic

parsley

olive oil

Wash the fish, coat them with flour and fry in hot oil in a paella dish or other wide pan, in batches if necessary, adding the mussels and clams last. When they are well cooked, set them aside and use the pan to make a sofregit, an onion and tomato sauce which is the basis of many a Catalan meal.

To do this, add more oil, heat through, then gently fry the chopped onions and add the tomatoes, slowly stirring and sautéeing until the liquid has evaporated and the tomatoes and onions make a sauce. Now throw in a glass of white wine, reduce for about three minutes, and add the fish stock. Simmer for around 12 minutes, then add the cooked fish. When the soup returns to the boil, lower the flame.

At the same time, make a picada by grinding together a small amount of saffron with two or three cloves of garlic, some salt and a couple of sprigs of parsley. Dissolve this paste in a small amount of the stock before adding it to the pan.

Throw in some brandy, dry sherry or Pernod if you feel like it, and cook for another 8-10 minutes. Serve with rice.

Crema catalana (Catalan burnt custard)

Catalonia's unique contribution to the Spanish dessert menu is this version of the French classic crème brûlée. Sometimes known as crema cremada (burnt cream), what sets it apart is its caramelised sugar crust. This recipe is taken from Catalan Cuisine by Colman Andrews, the standard work on the subject.

Serves 4

INGREDIENTS

500ml single cream

peel of half a lemon

half a cinnamon stick

3 egg yolks

170g sugar

Heat the cream, lemon peel and cinnamon stick in a saucepan over a medium heat until just boiling, then remove from the heat, discard the lemon peel and cinnamon stick, and allow to cool.

Beat the egg yolks with a third of the sugar until thick, then strain the cooled cream into the eggs, stirring constantly as you go.

Reheat the custard mixture in a heavy-bottomed saucepan over a low heat, stirring

▲ *Crema catalana*

constantly until it thickens slightly and coats the back of a wooden spoon. Allow it to cool slightly, then pour into individual ramekins or serving bowls.

Once the custard has set, sprinkle each serving with a layer of sugar and caramelise it until it is dark amber in colour. This is best done with a red-hot poker or a branding iron specially made for the purpose, but it can also be done under a very hot grill provided that the serving bowls are heat-proof.

An alternative method is to line a baking sheet with foil and butter, then sprinkle the sugar evenly in four circles of about the same diameter as the bowls, and grill for five minutes until the sugar has browned. Once the sugar has cooled, it can be peeled from the foil and placed on top of each serving of custard.

Published by Thomas Cook Publishing
Thomas Cook Holdings Ltd
PO Box 227
Thorpe Wood
Peterborough PE3 6PU
United Kingdom

Telephone: 01733 503571
Email: books@thomascook.com

Text © 2001 Thomas Cook Publishing
Maps © 2001 Thomas Cook Publishing

ISBN 1 841570 52 4

Distributed in the United States of
America by the Globe Pequot Press,
PO Box 480, Guilford, Connecticut
06437, USA

Publisher: Donald Greig
Commissioning Editor: Deborah Parker
Map Editor: Bernard Horton

Project management: Dial House
    Publishing
Series Editor: Christopher Catling
Copy Editor: Lucy Thomson
Proofreader: Joanne Hockin

Series and cover design: WhiteLight
Cover artwork: WhiteLight and
    Kaarin Wall
Text layout: SJM Design Consultancy,
    Dial House Publishing
Maps prepared by Polly Senior
    Cartography

Repro and image setting: PDQ Digital
    Media Solutions Ltd
Printed and bound in Italy by
    Eurografica SpA

Written and researched by **Tony Kelly**

We would like to thank Neil Setchfield for
the photographs used in this book, to
whom the copyright belongs.